DON'T FORGET TO PACK THE KIDS

(SHORT-TERM MISSIONS FOR YOUR WHOLE FAMILY)

Jill M. Richardson

Don't Forget to Pack the Kids

© 2012 Jill Marie Richardson, Revised 2013

BeachGlass Communications

All rights reserved. No part of this publication my be reproduced, stored in any retrieval system, or transmitted, in any for or by any means, without prior written permission of the author.

All Scripture references are New Living Translation, Tyndale House Publishers.

Cover photos by: Brent Richardson

Cover Design by: Emily Richardson

ISBN-13: 978-0615581187

ISBN-10: 0615581188

For Gerry and Sherry Chappeau, who first taught me what it meant not only to be a follower of Christ but to run after Him.

And for Nathan and Shannon, on the front lines of love.

Thank you, Resolution Church, for trusting me and "going with the flow." You're an awesome family.

About the Author

Jill has a BA in English and Education from Washington University in St. Louis and an MDiv in theology from Bethel University, St. Paul. She is an award-winning writer and speaker. Jill has published four books and numerous articles in and speaks in Chicago and surrounding areas.

She serves as an Associate Pastor at Resolution Church in Oswego, Illinois. Jill performs musical theater in her community, serving as a board member, director, and producer for Acorn Community Theater. She coaches the local junior high Battle of the Books team, is Vice President of her library board, and plays counselor, coach, and referee to three daughters.

Contact Jill at:

jillmarierichardson.com
https://www.facebook.com/jillwrites
http://jill-theimperfectjourney.blogspot.com
https://twitter.com/JillMarieRichar
http://pinterest.com/jimari/

TABLE OF CONTENTS

Introduction — Why?	8
Chapter 1 — Open Eyes	12
Chapter 2 — Head and Shoulders	17
Chapter 3 — And Some Final Reasons	25
Chapter 4 — Why Not?	35
Chapter 5 — I Got It on the Internet, It Must Be True	42
Chapter 6 — Can't I Just Hire a Telemarketer?	53
Chapter 7 — Passports, and Shots, and Packing — Oh My!	64
Chapter 8 — Don't Ever Cross the Chopsticks	78
Chapter 9 — Reality Bites	96
Chapter 10 — Packing Jesus	106
Chapter 11 — You Can't Go Home Again	115
Appendix A — Spiritual Gift Inventory	120
Appendix B — Family Bible Study	129
Appendix C--Packing Lists	133
Appendix D--Sample Parental Approval Form	137
Appendix E--Budget Worksheet	139
Appendix F--Timeline Checklist	140
Appendix G--Testimony Tips	142
Appendix H--Sample Support Letter	144

Reviews of Don't Forget to Pack the Kids

"If you've ever considered taking a family mission trip, this is the book to read."

"This unique book should be required reading for anyone taking their family to minister abroad."

"A goal I have for my family is to take a short term mission trip. This book helped me to decide whether this was really something for our family to do. It would be very helpful for anyone who wants to explore the possibility and would be an excellent resource to prepare."

"This is not just a book; it is a life changing book, a challenge to any Christian, a nudge to every Christian family."

"Jill Richardson and her husband took all three of their children on an unforgettable mission trip, and everyone came home transformed in large and small dimensions. The tone of this extremely well-written book is conversational. The reader will find her advice to be thoroughly pragmatic, dished up with self-effacing humor. The whole book is baptized into a spiritual perspective that will be invaluable to a family that is considering a mission trip for the first time. Read Don't Forget to Pack the Kids for guidance in creating your own plan for a life-changing adventure in service to Christ and to people he loves."

"We all want to raise our children to be more than we ever imagined they could be. We all want them to out-do us. Jill Richardson put this in perspective for me while I read her book in a way I had not realized before."

Don't Forget to Pack the Kids looks like a short read, but I am here to warn you that this book will consume you entirely for more than just reading those pages. I loved this book. It was information that anyone can use even if they are not going on a mission. It was entertaining yet Spiritual at the same time. I really don't know how to explain it. I felt like I was there with them. You will just have to read the book."

"When I saw the title of this book, Don't Forget to Pack the Kids, and read the description, I knew this book could bless our family. I have occasionally thought that our family should participate in some form of missionary work. I wasn't sure what we could do. I now think that going on a short mission trip would be perfect. I highly recommend this book! I'm looking forward to making plans to take the children on a mission trip."

"Don't Forget to Pack the Kids is an exceptional little book for anyone contemplating taking a mission trip, especially when a family is involved. The personal stories are really beautiful and the advice about how to deal with the specific issues/concerns of taking your children on such a life experience are invaluable. It's a well organized guidebook and to anyone contemplating foreign or domestic missions: Read it! You will not be disappointed."

INTRODUCTION
WHY?

We didn't know we were on the crest of any wave. As our teenaged daughters will pathetically testify, their parents have rarely been on the forefront of anything "cutting edge." Honestly, I just learned how to use a smart phone. Yet ten years ago, a burning desire to get our kids' hands and feet dirty in the real world, joined with an innocent Google search, lit a fire we didn't know had yet to be kindled.

Then, however, the reaction of other people when we hinted our intention for a family mission trip to China was somewhat different.

"You're going where?"

"Are you sure you'll be safe?"

"Have you really thought this through?"

"Maybe you should try something smaller first . . . soup kitchens are nice . . ."

And the most common question (usually uttered in a tone that conveyed, "step away from the crazy woman") —"*Why?*"

A less than enthusiastic reception. Were we three seats short of a full flight to pack up three kids and travel halfway across the world with strangers just to help out in an orphanage? Did we really think our grade school-age kids could, and should, minister beside their parents so far from home—eating, sleeping, and (worse) going to the bathroom in strange places?

Well, yes. And the answers to all those other questions?

You're going where? We're going to China. All of us. Mom, Dad, three kids. Sixty-six hundred miles, by my reckoning. Remember when we were kids and we'd go out in the backyard with our shovel and tell everyone we were digging to China? We knew then it was all the way on the other side of the planet. We had no concept of sixteen hours by plane. With a six-year-old. (Still, a lot easier than by shovel.) But now, we also know how close it really is.

Are you sure you'll be safe? No, we're not. But then, I'm not sure I'll be safe every time I get in my car or walk to the mailbox. We *have* carefully chosen a stable country with no out-of-the-ordinary violence. Taken the necessary health precautions. But life isn't safe.

Have you really thought this through? Quite a bit. Probably not enough. Kind of like getting married—some things you just can't prepare enough for. You do your best and navigate the tough stuff when it comes.

Why? The answer to that will fill the next few chapters.

Short-term missions have traditionally been the province of singles, youth groups, and married-with-no-kids. Five years ago, few would have picked up a book about taking the family on a short-term mission. Now, well, *you* have, haven't you?

Now, more and more of us 30 and 40-somethings with kids are asking—why can't we do something meaningful for others *with* our kids? Why do we have to wait until they're teens and then and pack them off on a youth group trip? Why can't we let them experience using their gifts in ministry *now*? And why can't we discover those gifts alongside one another in an experience they'll never forget?

Well, you can. With some planning specifically geared toward making a family mission trip successful, you can. And you should. More families want to experience service *together* now rather than as a generationally-segregated adventure. More and more people don't want to wait until their kids are grown to fulfill some of their youthful idealistic dreams.

Volunteer vacation lectures have become "the next big thing" at travel conventions. Books have been written listing trip options. But parent need more than a book full of options. They need reasons, instructions, and encouragement. They need a long-term rationalization for what they are doing, why, and what they will do in the future. Christian families need something that addresses volunteerism from a spiritual standpoint rather than simply a do-good-feel-good idealism. To succeed and thrive in creating a service spirit, rather than simply taking a vacation with a little work thrown in, families need to plan more than the destination and cheap airfare. They need to plan a life-change adventure.

For the first four chapters of this book, we'll talk about the "to go or not to go" question. Through stories of our own experience, Scripture, and the input of experts in the field, we'll discover together the basis for jumping into this adventure.

Then, the mechanics. After the why—what about the How? That will consume the following six chapters.

Finally, the "What Now." The most important part of all.

One last point about the Where. Even though, as you read, you will hear about passports and customs and language barriers, you can apply almost all of this information to a domestic mission trip as well. A domestic trip, too, is every bit as "spiritual" as a foreign one—so you can jettison all those old "holy one-upmanship" plays other may have put in your head previously that stop you from going wherever you're sent—Appalachia to Argentina, Mongolia to Mississippi.

But . . . don't suppose you "won't need" any of the advice for foreign missions either. I absolutely guarantee you—if you venture form Pittsburgh to Pine Ridge, South Dakota, you'll experience just as much culture shock, just as many confusing customs, and just as much spiritual warfare as going from New York to Namibia. And yes, spending a week in an inner city only two hours from home can present a language barrier, too.

Why? So many reasons. Let me explain why we took our family on a short-term mission trip. In that explanation, perhaps you'll find the answers to some of your own questions.

CHAPTER ONE
OPEN EYES

Our almost-twelve-year-old daughter, Becca, rocked the Chinese baby slowly, back and forth, her voice low and soothing. "It's OK, Amber. You're OK with me. Such a sweet baby." She touched the infant's upper lip, gently but without hesitation. She traced the indentation there, a lip shaped in an odd way she'd never seen before. The deformity had caused this baby's mother to abandon her at a hospital, but it didn't offend her new champion. "How could anyone ever leave you? I wouldn't leave you. I love you, Amber."

My husband and I had talked about the idea of a short-term mission trip for three years, but it never seemed to feel quite right. Yet as our girls got older, I saw them adapting more and more to our relatively easy life in the suburbs. Most of the kids in their schools look, dress, and think alike. Most live in well-above-average homes. For those willing to pay (and most around here are), every want and need can be found within a fifteen-minute drive.

Yes, we went to church every week and learned the evils of sin, but what about the evils of complacency? I feared that our culture of prosperity and instant gratification would slowly numb them into being careless Christians, unaware of and unconcerned with the hurting world beyond their comfortable lives.

I don't want them to grow up believing that living counter to their culture just means a checklist of do's and don't's. I don't want them to believe that if they buy fair trade coffee and bring in reusable shopping bags they can feel god about themselves and check out of more intimate investment. My wish for them is that their investment costs them something. They need to comprehend Mother Teresa's words:

"Love cannot remain by itself--it has no meaning. Love has to be put into action, and that action is service. . . . Let us not be satisfied with just giving money. Money is not enough, money can be got, but they need your hearts to love them."

Why did we go to China? I wanted my children's hearts to be captured in such as way that they could not ever look at their own world through the same eyes. And looking, they would not be satisfied without doing something to change it.

Being countercultural shouldn't be news for Christians. Jesus sent us "into the world" (John 17:18) yet maintained that we were "not of this world" (John 17:16). For 2,000 years, we've been trying to puzzle through exactly what that means. Not only what He meant, but how to apply that meaning in every generation.

In the early church, it required refraining from pagan sexual practices and idolatry. It also motivated early Christians to care for the poor, orphaned, widowed, sick, and enslaved with sacrifices their "world" could not understand.

In our age, being "in the world but not of it" has become a cliché. "Not of" translates almost always into a list of things Christians shouldn't do in order to "prove" they're Christians. For most of the things on our list of "thou shalt nots," there is wisdom in not doing them. It's not a bad list.

The problem with lists is that, when we make one, we think we've got the requirements for the test down. We believe we can get an A with God if we just complete the list. That's what the rich young ruler thought. But God wanted an entirely different view of "in the world but not of it" from this young man.

"Someone came to Jesus with this question: 'Teacher, *what good things must I do* to have eternal life?' Jesus told him, 'If you want to be perfect, go and sell all you have and give the money to the poor, and you will have treasure in heaven. Then come, follow me.' But when the young man heard this, he went sadly away because he had many possessions." (Matthew 19:16, 21-22)

Jesus offers this advice to the young man—Quit making lists. Quite trying to follow the rules. Actually, try breaking some. Try showing the world that something else entirely has gotten hold of your heart. Try showing them what it's like to love God more than any thing in this life.

The message didn't sit well with the young man. If Jesus walked through the suburbs of Chicago where we live, it wouldn't sit well here either. I'm glad our kids have grown up knowing Christians try to steer away from lifestyles that can harm them. But I don't want them to grow up believing that living counter to their culture just means avoiding premarital sex and violent video games. I want them to see how their particular culture seeps into *every part* of their lives. I want them to understand that what their peers believe about the world can affect the central values of their lives, values they don't even realize they're forming.

We know how our kids feel about drugs, alcohol, and spending their life savings in Vegas. At least, we know what we've taught them. But do we know how they feel about having too much *stuff*? If they know when enough is enough? Their convictions about confronting racism or championing the discarded? Do we know if they feel entitled to what they want when they want it? Do we comprehend the pressures to be beautiful, athletic, and perfect—and the values these pressures create?

This is the culture we wanted our kids to begin consciously running counter to. Being "not of the world" around here means living values that aren't all about getting more, buying bigger, overscheduling, and overachieving. I suspect that's what the world looks like to a lot of people reading this book as well.

Why take our kids on a mission trip? To open their eyes to a world where the values they see around them daily at home appear for what they are—false gods. Meaningless chasing of the wind. To encourage them to live as if something—or someone—else entirely has gotten hold of their hearts.

"It's time to go back to the hotel, Becca." I peeked into the nursery doorway and whispered so as not to disturb Amber.

"I don't want to leave her, Mom."

"She's sleeping, sweetheart. You can put her in bed. We'll be back."

Becca looked at the sleeping child. "When will she have her surgery?" The orphanage now routinely funded the surgery for cleft palates.

"I don't know. I don't know how old they have to be. They say the babies come out of the surgeries with hardly a scar. They'll make her little mouth beautiful."

"I don't want to leave her."

"I know."

"Mom?" She set the little girl gently into the crib.

"What?"

"She's already beautiful."

CHAPTER TWO
HEAD AND SHOULDERS

Encouraging my kids to run counter cultural doesn't stop at the church doors, either. One part of our culture that also disturbed us squatted right there in the church. As our kids sank into compliance with it, too, we knew we needed to show them an alternative.

"And now, dear brothers and sisters, I will write about the special abilities the Holy Spirit gives to each of us. Now there are different kinds of spiritual gifts, but it is the same Holy Spirit who is the source of them all. There are different kinds of service in the church, but it is the same Lord we are serving. There are different ways God works in our lives, but it is the same God who does the work through all of us. A spiritual gift is given to each of us as a means of helping the entire church." (1 Corinthians 12:1,4-7)

Generally, evangelicals accept and embrace the gifts of the Holy Spirit (though we differ, perhaps, on what they are). In most churches, however, we encourage and train only the gifts of the *adults* in our body. Children learn early that they have two tasks in the church—be educated and be entertained. Both are passive tasks. They learn that "mom and dad and the pastor" can and will handle all that other stuff while they watch.

One billion people on the planet report their goings on on Facebook regularly. Twenty-five million "pin" their likes and dislikes. Fifty million tweet about anything that fits into 140 characters, and 150 million experience the visual kaleidoscope that is tumblr.

What do all these statistics mean? Well, for one thing they mean we're connecting to a lot of people and having an electronic fiesta in our daily lives. Yet some things about this technological party feel wrong. Among them, at gut level, is the realization that so much of what we do in a day is *all about us*. What we like, don't like, look like, feel like. What we're doing, listening to, or eating. And, it's all about sitting still and letting the world feed us what we like. It's passive and narcissistic at its worst. It's a world we love--but it's a world in which we must teach our children healthy navigation skills.

I don't want my kids to grow up believing their environment owes them a perpetual spoon in the mouth and drink in hand. I want them to seek to give input, not continually get it. I hope they will learn to employ themselves in making what's happening happen, not just retweeting it.

"A pessimist, they say, sees a glass of water as being half empty; an optimist sees the same thing as half full. But a giving person sees a glass of water and starts looking for someone who might be thirsty." G. Donald Gale

I want the kid who is looking, not just commenting on the glass of water. But if I don't encourage my child to discover her gifts and to exercise them, how do I know she will want to exercise them as an adult? How do I know she won't always expect church to passively entertain her?

I've not yet read the Scripture that said children had to wait and watch until they're old enough to "handle" using their gifts. In fact, I've read in several passages how God *did* use children who had been trained to listen and obey. We felt our children needed to experience their faith in action, discovering that they didn't have to grow up before they could be ministers.

"Some children were brought to Jesus so he could lay his hands on them and pray for them. The disciples told them not to bother him. But Jesus said, 'Let the children come to me. Don't stop them! For the kingdom of heaven belongs to such as these.' And he put his hands on their heads and blessed them before he left." (Matthew 19:13-15)

Usually, we focus on the bumbling of the disciples in that story. But I am a writer, so I can't help always asking the question—what happens next? And I really want to hear the end of this particular story.

What do you suppose those children *did* after experiencing Jesus so intimately? Ran and played on the beach like nothing had happened? Went off and asked mom what was for lunch? OK, some probably did. But my guess is, others couldn't wait to tell someone about the amazing man they'd met who treated them with respect and acted like they were his most precious treasure on earth. I think they spread the news faster than an updated Facebook status. I think they were—*ministers*.

If we truly believe the Scripture that tells us the Holy Spirit has given gifts to all believers, why can a six-year-old not learn to use those gifts as well as an adult? We thought she could, and should. Yes, at six those gifts aren't yet clear, but why not begin exploring what they might be? And heck, why not in China?

The Chinese teenager pointed at us, put her hands to her mouth, then let her fingers flow out and down, almost like blowing a kiss. She spoke in quick Mandarin.

"She says, 'We sang for you, now you sing for us,'" the leader translated. "Teach us an English song."

Besides working in the orphanage, we had also come to China to help students in area schools practice English. According to the design, as they began to ask questions about us, we could share why we were there and what we believed. But what song could we teach? The girls lined up in a circle around us, expectant.

"I know, I know!" cried Emily, our 10-year-old. "Head and shoulders, knees and toes!" she began singing loudly, vigorously using the accompanying motions.

At home, we constantly pester Emily to turn down the volume. Too loud, too fast, too quick to act impulsively. But here . . . the group had needed an energetic song leader. Emily did on impulse what the adults could not figure out how to do. All eyes watched our tall middle child and copied her hand movements, touching their head, shoulders, knees, and toes in time to the words.

We wanted our girls to be ministers *now*. Couldn't they do that at home? Yes, but the distractions of daily life pull all of us away from a focus on using our gifts for others. For kids, the whole vague concept of ministering competes poorly with the buzz of here and now. On a mission trip where they know they're part of the team, they focus. There are no distractions. Their sole purpose for two weeks is being active in ministry, not passive receptacles.

Research tells us that 75 percent of young people in our churches today will leave them when they leave home. Why? Because they increasingly believe that church is irrelevant to their daily lives and out of touch with the culture. In other words, they don't see the point. And in ever-busier lives, everything we spend our time on has to have a point.

What would happen if, instead, our churches taught kids from the time they could walk that they were ministers? That they were the hands and feet to *make* the church relevant? That the ends of the earth weren't as far away or impossible to impact as they thought? I truly believe we could turn those statistics upside down.

Tinkling Chinese laughter mixed with exhausted whoops of older team members as we all finished the song with gusto.

"Head, shoulders, knees, toes," one girl pointed as she proudly spoke four new English words. "Another?"

"Umm, how about . . . "Emily launched into Deep and Wide, slowly at first so the girls could learn the words. Two songs. 17 new English words. Singing about Jesus in a communist-run middle school. Led by a 10-year-old. A minister of Christ.

OPEN ARMS

For Christmas the year of the trip, we gave Becca a card from Samaritan's Purse that read, "A gift was given in honor of Becca to provide loving care for orphans." I watched her eyes get moist and I knew that, much as she loved the new "Rippin' Rocket Roller Coaster" set she had opened first, she would have traded it for that card. These orphans are not pictures on a flyer or names pulled off a web site.

For our girls, these children on the other side of the planet have faces and names. As one of our most significant goals for the trip, we wanted our children to become world Christians who truly understood the question of the Good Samaritan—who is my neighbor?

Americans suffer from "compassion fatigue"—too many disasters, too many people to help—so too many do nothing at all out of paralysis. We want to help when hurricanes, tornadoes, and tsunamis strike. But the task seems overwhelming for one person and figuring out how to help too complex. Even putting aside disasters and considering the millions in hunger daily—what can one busy person possibly do?

Again we found Becca in the orphanage nursery. She held Grace, the newest arrival. She, too, had a cleft palate and so had been deposited on the orphanage doorstep. For most of its existence, this place has taken in older children orphaned, abandoned, or living with people unable to care for them. But as they gained a reputation for caring for the least of these, on their doorstep had begun to appear babies, left by women who knew someone would care for them behind those walls.

"How could anyone leave a baby?"

"I don't know, sweetheart. There are so many reasons we can't understand."

"They could only have one, and she wasn't perfect." Sadness at a reality way beyond her nearly 12 years filled her voice.

"Sometimes," I nodded. "Or they knew they couldn't afford the medical care to help her. She'd never be accepted the way she is."

"Right." Already, Becca knew this tragic fact of the culture. A defect would brand this child an outcast for life.

"So maybe her mother loved her very much—enough to give her away to someone who could help her."

"But that's wrong. Mothers shouldn't have to leave their little girls."

"Yeah, I know. That's why we're here."

"But what can we do?"

Pastor Eric Spangler of Mobilization for Free Methodist World Missions, explains why he took his children, ages four to twelve, to India. "We hoped our children would gain a larger perspective of the world and the kingdom of God, as well as a sense for the lives of those who suffer."

What is a world Christian? It is a person whose sense of brotherhood and sisterhood—personal connection—knows no boundaries of color, nationality, or religion. A world Christian doesn't consider starvation in Africa or religious persecution in Nepal something that happens to "them" rather than to us. She knows every statistic is a human being for whom Christ died. And a world Christian never lets the question of what can one person do stop him or her from doing what one person can.

"What are you doing, Becca?"
"I'm just holding her."
"If you weren't here, who would hold this one baby?"
"But I'll leave."
"Does it make a difference to her that you are here, now?"
Grace smiled and gurgled as Becca dangled a toy before her eyes. Becca smiled. "I guess so. I guess it matters to her."

We want world Christian children who just happen to be North American and white. We want kids who feel a personal connection with kids across the globe. Maybe then, a lot of "one persons" who feel helpless can get together to do what one person can't do.

By the way, that tall middle child? She just spent three months in Guatemala without us. She didn't need us anymore to know she could look for someone who was thirsty.

She also just spent two weeks helping lead three younger girls through their first missions experience, processing their feelings of inadequacy alongside the dirt floors, lack of food, and teen mothers we met in Costa

Rica. She watched their hearts be broken, as hers had been, and she led them through the process of opening those hearts and arms further than the girls had believed possible. The ten-year-old missionary is making disciples.

God promised Abraham that his offspring would be as numerous as the stars. There are approximately seventy sextillion stars in the *known* universe (that's seven followed by 22 zeroes). There are no national boundaries, no skin colors, no houses that look better or lawns greener than anyone else's among the stars. When we look at the stars, they all look pretty much alike to us.

That's the way God wants us to look at his human creations, too. Revelation tells us that John, "Saw a vast crowd, too great to count, from every nation and tribe and people and language, standing in front of the throne and before the Lamb. They were clothed in white and held palm branches in their hands. And they were shouting with a mighty shout, 'Salvation comes from our God on the throne and from the Lamb.'" (Revelation 7:9-10)

That's one party I can't wait to be invited to. A sea of tongues, cultures, and races all united for one purpose — praising God. I ache to see that unity. Until then, I want my kids to understand — the whole world is invited to the party. We should get to know them now.

CHAPTER THREE
AND SOME FINAL REASONS

OPEN AGENDAS

From the first "squatty potty" when we got off the plane to the fish head on a platter, the girls realized—things are different here. Since forgoing the bathroom for two weeks was not an option, they had to adapt. Children who at home will argue over who sat in the front seat the day before yesterday can display astounding flexibility in a foreign country.

Let me tell you right now, our kids have a tough time with "adapting." They do not like change. Witness the howls of outrage when we suggested going away for Easter weekend. Not because the idea was a bad one, but because, in our girls' eyes, you just don't mess with the way Easter is and always has been. Forever and ever amen.

Put the same three girls in a foreign country on a mission. Tell them the language is different, the food is different, the transportation is different, the stores and schools are different, and the bathrooms *definitely* are different, and their response is . . . "cool." (Well, except for the bathrooms. Very *not* cool. But they did adapt.)

"Come, come," the young merchant lady beckoned Beth, our youngest. "You sit."

Beth glanced at me and, assured I wouldn't abandon her at the barrette booth in Red Gate Shopping Market, smiled at the two ladies and sat on their stool. Out came two combs, and the ladies began combing and caressing her waist-length light brown hair.

"Oooh."
"Pretty."
"You have beautiful hair."

They ooohed and aaahed alternately as they combed, delighted at this wonder before them, thrilled just to play with hair of a color and texture they had never seen.

This is the child who, at home, gives me approximately 35 seconds to comb her hair, I thought. Beth never sat still that long. She'd also never been so comfortable with strangers. Only six, she appeared to know how happy she could make them just by sitting there.

"So pretty," the woman said again as Beth stood up to go. She pinned a white flower in my daughter's hair. "You keep," she told me, pointing at the floral barrette. She meant it. A fair trade for the enjoyment, in her eyes. I bought another anyway. We walked on through the market, my baby and me, her now-shiny, combed hair swinging at her waist.

Normally shy and fearful, our youngest found herself the center of attention everywhere. Most people had never seen a little pale-skinned girl with long brown hair. Beth just smiled, shrugged, and accepted the crowds of children pressing her with gifts in every classroom we visited.

She accepted the TV crew that pursued her and photographed her through our tour of a former landowner's mansion. She accepted the kids who, at our first school, swarmed her so thoroughly I could not get a glimpse of my daughter for at least fifteen minutes. Sure I would find her quivering and near tears afterward, instead I saw her seated on a desk like a princess, gracefully bestowing her smiles and fingertips on everyone.

I worried often that Beth's timid personality would be completely overwhelmed. After all, having a strange woman grab you in Tienanmen Square and place you (not ask, *place* you) in her family picture can be a bit unnerving for anyone, let alone a little girl who has been known to ask me sixteen times in one morning if I'm *sure* I'll remember to pick her up after school. Yet somehow, knowing she was doing something important allowed her to adapt with graciousness and poise I wish I always possessed.

Colleges, workplaces, and governments all recognize the value of an education in adaptability. Increasingly, people will have no choice but to develop it, as their environment changes in exponential fashion. If you don't see the value in teaching your kids to "go with the flow," consider the belief of the National Advisory Committee on Creative and Cultural Education:

"Adult learning will in future take place in a world where flexibility and adaptability are required in the face of new, strange, complex, risky and changing situations; where there are diminishing numbers of precedents and models to follow; where we have to work on the possibilities as we go along."

The Easter debacle notwithstanding, learning to adapt on a mission trip gave our kids some of the confidence they need to adapt at home as well. Hard as change at home can be, they know now they've faced harder. (They hardly blinked at the fish head for dinner). They still might not *want* to, but they know they can.

Ten years later, on our latest trip to Costa Rica, our team of fifteen struggled to accept the fact that we did not hit the ground running right out of the airport. Our hosts had no concrete plan. They assured us they would make it up as soon as we arrived. And--we waited. Knowing the culture, I did not find this surprising or disturbing. For task-oriented Americans, however, adaptability to that scenario wasn't easy. For three kids who had started this sort of odyssey ten years before, it didn't mean frustration--it meant time to explore. When the best-laid plans did not go as expected? Just adapt.

OPEN MINDS

All the men in our group gathered around the vintage red convertible in mint condition. Someone would get the privilege of riding with our host in his car to the television station where we were to be honored guests at a live show. Every man in the group wanted to sit in that car. All I could think of was—no seat belts. No roof. Chinese driving. Bad combo. No thanks.

Then our team leader (a *serious* car aficionado) informed us—the host had offered the privileged ride to the three children of the group. *My* children. In a speeding, swerving, honking, seatbeltless car with a strange man. God, take me home now, this has got to be that line I cannot cross. But we knew the dilemma. Refusal would be insulting. It would cause our host to feel shamed and would damage our mission there. We would be ugly Americans. *Christian* ugly Americans.

We let them go, while the rest of us packed into two seatless cabs and I prayed throughout the entire trip. In letting them go, we broke nearly every rule they knew from home. Why? Because to hold on to our culture, our rules, and our expectations would have been to squash his. We couldn't do that and remain ambassadors for Christ.

China was the first time our older girls had been struck with the stunning realization—not everyone thinks the way we do. And sometimes, when thought patterns and rules of others run so contrary to ours and we run the risk of breaking tenuous fellowship, we'd better learn to bend. In other words—cultural sensitivity.

Not having really seen that many other cultures BC—Before China—the girls naturally believed theirs the gold standard. Now, not only do they understand sensitivity to others' standards, they recognize that these different cultures are in fact all around them here at home. Just because someone has white skin doesn't mean her "culture" may not be worlds away from your own. Through the experience of caring more about their mission in China than their "norms," the girls practiced caring more at home, too.

OPEN HEARTS

"Eat your broccoli. There are starving children in China." No, I can honestly say that cliche has never passed my lips, but I certainly remember hearing it as a child. It didn't have a whole lot of impact on most of us when our parents tried it, did it? Hungry children in a far-off land had little tangible meaning for us.

I'll never have to use that phrase on my children—they know. They've seen them. And the effect of seeing them may not cause them to clean their plates any better than I did 40 years ago (though my kids actually *like* vegetables), but its ripple effect goes way beyond broccoli.

We hugged Jenny as we left the orphanage for the last time. Jenny's quick smile, willingness to hold our hands, and curious eyes had charmed our whole family in China. We unanimously voted that, if we could bring one child home in a suitcase with us, it would be Jenny. Her story made those bright eyes even more amazing.

A 42-year-old junk man found Jenny in a sewage ditch. He thought she was about a year old when he found her. He also found and cared for a young boy. They lived in an 8x8-foot cave with no electricity, water, or heat. The man seemed kind, the orphanage officials said, but his mental capacity made it difficult for him to care for Jenny. Her hair was so matted upon arrival it had to all be cut off. In "survival" mode for some time after arriving at the orphanage, Jenny had to slowly learn that there would always be food, and love, to go around.

Teaching kids gratitude for what they have is a great byproduct of a missions trip. But be careful—as a primary motive for going in the first place, it stinks. (See Chapter 4.) If your kids are like ours, they have too much stuff and they want more. Kids (and adults) have a very difficult time distinguishing between wants and needs, as well as resisting the immediate gratification itch. On a missions trip, they will see their definition of "needs" drastically challenged.

In China we met kids living in caves. We saw farmers manually hoeing their fields in the hot sun. We met a boy thrown into a river to die because of his birth defect. We even met a whole orphanage full of kids who were (gasp!) *grateful* for the chance to go to school. It sent our kids' well-ordered "everything I want is only a mall away" world into a tailspin.

But when kids encounter the real needs of other people, no one responds more sincerely and more completely. Kids, so generous by nature, begin to put themselves in the supply and demand equations they had always assumed were part of the grown-up world. They realize — *I* can do without new shoes, McDonald's, another DVD — in order to allow someone who has less to have more.

A missions trip is no magic pill to make our children (or us) permanently grateful for all we have. They will still pine for the right clothes, newest electronics, or take-out food. (After all, so will you.) But they won't easily forget what they'll see, and it will influence future choices.

Beyond even the material things, however, our kids soon saw that other more profound differences existed for which they could give thanks. The children in the orphanage we visited were not female Chinese babies, as most people assumed. They were children of all ages with various reasons for being there. Some had been truly orphaned. Some were abandoned because of a birth defect or second marriage. Some lived with grandparents or relatives too elderly and impoverished to care for them. Some were just alone and couldn't even remember why.

All had one thing in common — no safety net. When they lost a parent who cared for them, they lost everything. I didn't realize that our kids were even processing this until one of them asked me one day, "Mom, what will happen to us if you and Dad die?"

"You will go to Aunt Cami and Uncle Peter's."
"Are you sure?"
"Yes, everyone in both families knows that. It's arranged."
"How would we get there?"

"You've got Grandma and Grandpa and all your aunts and uncles. They'll be here in an instant."

"Oh. Mom—we're lucky."

Still further comes another wonderfully unexpected area of gratitude—gratitude for their faith. The orphans' stories caused us to wrestle with many a question about man's inhumanity to man.

Emily raced along the banks of the Yellow River doing what she did best—keeping up with the boys. Their impromptu game of tag complete, one young boy and Em flopped down to enjoy some shade. I focused and shot to capture the smiling pair.

"That's Henry," the orphanage owner told us. "His smile is something special to see."

Henry, we learned, had been passed from relative to relative, never wanted in one place or staying there for too long. His double cleft palate made him a bad omen for his family and the butt of cruel and inhumane teasing from his peers. The last relative to have Henry shuffled off upon him decided the most "merciful" thing to do would be to throw him in the river and leave him to die.

Seeing the boy, an elderly woman waded into the river and rescued him. Despite her poverty and near blindness, she raised him as best she could until the orphanage offered to give him a home complete with schooling and adequate food. They also provided the surgery to fix Henry's smile.

Many of the other kids' stories had similar themes, if not so horrible in detail. *How?* our girls wanted to know over and over. How?

The seemingly inexplicable behavior of others does not need to lead to hang wringing and appalled disbelief. It can lead to some of the most profitable discussions with your kids--what do we as a family believe? About life and its value, about mercy and compassion, about humanity and inhumanity? Especially, what difference does *God* make?

When will these conversations happen in the normal course of your daily life? At home, we can run away from them or distract ourselves from their impact. But if we choose not to, because they're staring us in the face, we discover their intense value.

How does what you believe influence how you act? If there is no God, what difference does it make how we treat one another? If God is only a god to be feared and appeased, where do love and grace fit in? How does faith change a person? How does Christianity, which proclaims that we are made in the image of God and God would even give his life for us, compare with what you see in a culture that doesn't know Him? What is it really like to live without the hope of Jesus?

In a world where our children are taught that one religion is as good as another, coming face-to-face with the real-life (and death) implications of another belief system can shatter that feeble myth.

Everyone's questions notwithstanding, we boarded the plane that October for an adventure together that I believe changed our children more than it did the adults. Why short-term missions? So many reasons. Maybe something our youngest daughter wrote at the start of our last mission trip to Costa Rica can summarize:

"I kind of just always felt called to mission work. I'm so thankful and lucky to have been on a mission trip when I was only six. It opened my eyes to how different the world can be. I saw different cultures, and while I may have only been six and not really understood why we were there or

what we were doing, I just remember smiling the whole trip and helping others be happier. Without that trip, I have no idea if I would be the same person I am today. I've always just loved being there to do whatever. To listen, to offer advice, to help out in any way. I definitely want to continue just being there for people. I want to be the kind of person that people come to whenever they need something."

CHAPTER FOUR
WHY NOT?

There's a lot of debate about the value of short-term missions. Does the trip most benefit the people in the country you're helping or the people who go? Do families or teams really make a long-term impact on the place? Wouldn't the resources used to send them be more effective given to the people in the country to help themselves?

Mathematically, short-term missions don't add up. If you go somewhere for two weeks, you won't change the world. Not yet, anyway. Yes, the people themselves could use that money more efficiently, if all you're looking at is immediate practical return on investment. But I think that's a wrong way to look at things. You need an eternal, long-term vantage.

If you weigh the precise value of sending a six-year-old to China, you won't get a return on your investment that you can quantify. What you will get is a kid who grows up who loves better, cares more, and is determined to make a difference. You have no idea how far-reaching that will be. You have a family on fire for missions returning to a home church and refusing to let things be business as usual. Done wrong, yes it can be damaging.

Done right, it can have a ripple effect that no one sees the end of.

In fact, I do believe the short-term benefit is mainly on the side of those who go, not those they serve. But I do *not* believe that is a bad thing. And I do not believe we need to apologize for it. Why not? Because I strongly believe that the *long-term* effects of changing, and challenging, a handful of peoples' worldview are profound and will have a greater positive impact on the rest of the world than we have any idea. The effect, particularly on children, can be exponential.

The good news—most agency leadership with whom I spoke for this book couldn't think of reasons they would disqualify a family from going a mission trip. So, no matter how messed up you think your family unit may be, chances are, it's not as bad as you think. If you'll work with them, they'll do their best to work with you. Bad news—if you do go, even when you see so many red flags waving ahead of you it looks like a Chinese New Year's Parade, you risk more damage than you really know.

Is a mission trip right for your family? Better to ask the tough questions before you go than when you're staring at that squid soup and wondering how you strayed so far from Kansas.

Question Number 1 — What do I expect?

Expect to get tired. Expect to get sick. Expect to get confused. Expect to feel incredibly like a dumb American at times. If none of that happens, you lucked out. Be blessed. If (when) it does and you went expecting continual blessing and euphoric mountaintop experiences, the reverse won't feel so blessed. A mission trip *is* a mountaintop, life-changing experience. But it isn't that 24 hours a day for two weeks. Sometimes, it's diarrhea, and jet lag, and sharing 24-inch train bunks.

Hmmm, we realized, as we stashed our suitcases under the beds in the train from Beijing to Henan. This will definitely not be an Amtrak. The beds of our semi-private sleeper car came down from both sides of the wall, about 24 inches wide with mattresses that looked thinner than a disposable baby-changing pad in the restroom. Not to mention there were five of us and four of them.

I suddenly remembered my complete inability to sleep with any other person touching any part of my body and wondered how this would work. Someone knocked on our semi-private door. Laura, one of the single women on our trip, stood there looking apprehensive.

"Um, I'm in the room next door. Alone. I got put in there with three strange men, and, well, they're strange . . . I'm afraid to go to sleep," she finished. A faithful, uncomplaining servant, she had every right to decide this sacrifice was asking too much. Still, she held back from asking if she could fit in with us for the night. Of course she could. The 10 and 11-year-old sisters snuggled in one bunk, the six-year-old climbed in with me, and we prepared for the eight-hour overnight ride.

But I had forgotten one thing. Beth moves in her sleep. A lot. Stopping with the screeching brakes and the glaring lights of another station every half-hour didn't help. "Sleeper car" was definitely a misnomer. No sleep happened that night in my half of the cot.

Would I trade that sleepless night for one at the Ritz-Carlton? No, I would not. How many people can say they've experienced a Chinese sleeper train? The richness of having the experience far outweighs the discomfort, though when my darling daughter's knees jabbed my back at 3 am and I had to feel my way in the jolting dark to the "bathroom" at the end of the car, well, I may not have been so easily convinced.

Great Expectations can ruin more than freshman English lit class. Unrealistic dreams of saving the world while retaining all the comforts of home will bring you to a crash landing sooner than a Cessna piloted by three-year-old. Do you know the first rule of missions? *Be flexible*. Read it. Memorize it. Understand it. Tattoo it on your forehead, if necessary. Go, with the expectation that the experience will alter your expectations. That the place will change you more than you will change the place. That God may not do what you expect but will always do what you need.

Question Number 2 — Why am I going?

Motives for taking a family mission trip vary for everyone. They may change, be inconsistent, even feel quite selfish at times. I struggled myself with the motivation factor. One major purpose for me was to allow our children to see how the rest of the world lived. I wanted them to recognize their pampered suburban life as the privilege it was and develop the compassionate willingness to sacrifice.

But that motive seemed so "unspiritual" when I read the books and web sites that talked about going "only for God's glory." If I wanted something for *me* on this trip, if I wasn't wholly motivated by God's glory and service — was I dooming my family to a scarlet "S" for selfish that everyone on the team would see?

You can have many motives for pursuing a short-term mission, and those which entail a benefit to you don't have to be suspect or second-class. Why *wouldn't* God want to use the experience to help your family grow? Is He not capable of blessing both sides of the equation at once (servant and servee)? God is the original multitasker; He can work with all your motivations—at least all the ones you submit to him.

If your goals include helping your children and yourself be better people—more compassionate, more informed, more willing—those are God's goals for you as well. Don't be ashamed of wanting them because they sound less holy than just "going for the kingdom."

Yet, sometimes our motivations for personal change don't come from such a pure place. "I want my kids to see how fortunate they are," differs quite a bit from "I want my kids to stop whining about what they don't have and be grateful, darn it." "I want my son to learn to use his spiritual gifts," does not equal "I want my teenager to get off his butt and do something."

Appropriate and inappropriate motives for taking your kids differ subtly. The first endeavors to nourish your kids and help them grow and learn. It's what we want them to do and be. The other focuses on what we want them to *stop* doing—extinguishing bad behavior or attitudes with a healthy dose of spiritual sacrifice. Though God can work with the latter, he usually chooses not to. Something about that tricky free will thing. Bottom line—are you going to nourish a child's spirit or to straighten a child out? Be sure you know the answer to that question before you sign the forms.

Along the same lines, don't go to straighten out a spouse or marriage, either. What makes you think a relationship that's tenuous at home will improve over two weeks of close quarters, confusing surroundings, and unusual demands? Not to mention the nightmare team bonding could become when everyone sees you two facing off. A mission trip is *not* a panacea for family ills. The same petri dish can grow a deadly bacteria or life-saving penicillin—depending on what's put into it. So can two weeks in the field. So—put something positive in the dish if you want a positive result.

Question Number 3—Is your family perfect?

That said, please don't believe you need a perfect family. A year before we went to China, our oldest child was diagnosed with Tourette syndrome. All three girls have struggled with varying degrees of ADD, TS, or OCD. (You can see why I at first considered a 16-hour plane ride nothing short of five tickets to purgatory.) We knew the stress of a strange place and people would probably bring their hyperactivity and impulse control issues full-court. On the other hand, these kinds of kids are thrill seekers, so foreign travel hooked them quickly.

Yet rather than disqualify them from short-term missions, their "unusual" attributes worked overseas. Becca, so deeply sensitive, held the precious babies like they'd never known. She asked the tough questions about their abandonment, and we could see the resolve growing her never to forget to care. Emily, the loud and the wild, became a natural leader among the group of children. Wherever she went, kids gathered.

Crucial to this success, however, was honest communication with the team leader. He knew before he met us about our particular challenges and what to expect (although the hallmark of TS and ADD is—you never know what to expect!). Team members supported us, took the kids off for expeditions to give us breaks, and acted with more acceptance and understanding than church members who had known us for years. The moral —don't be scared off by a family with "issues" or disabilities. But *do* be honest and communicate with your team.

So . . .

Don't go if:

—You feel you owe it to God. (He likes to be paid in love, not guilt.)

—You feel you owe it to your pastor/friend/coworker/dog. Someone else's calling to go is not yours.

—To straighten out a bad kid/marriage.

—Because you've always wanted to see the Caribbean. (You will not be a tourist on a mission trip. You'll be so much more.)

—It's the last thing on earth your kids want to do. Unwilling family members can drag down everyone's effectiveness. Make sure everyone is on board.

—You expect comfort and the status quo.

Don't stay home if:

—You're not perfect.

—You're not a spiritual giant.

—You have normal worries and fears.

—You're not the most talented, most extroverted, most capable person for the job.

—God wants you to go.

CHAPTER FIVE
I GOT IT ON THE INTERNET, IT MUST BE TRUE
(FINDING A TRIP)

The Perfect Start

Okay, so maybe we didn't use the most sensible method of choosing a trip, but it worked. I simply googled. Well, not really simply, but still, not exactly thoroughly researched. An Internet search for short-term missions turned up hundreds of opportunities. We live in a big, needy world, and the options can overwhelm a first-time seeker. A family, however, would be wise to determine their unique parameters to narrow the search. I tested the possibilities with three basic questions.

1) Does the mission accept families? Most did not. That eliminated quite a few choices immediately. You need to search for a group that specifically encourages families, not just adults and teens. If they'll consider the idea only reluctantly, you may want to look elsewhere for your first trip.

2) Can all family members participate in ministry? Everyone assumed we would choose a medical mission for my husband to best use his skills. But a family mission trip is about the family skills, not just the parents'. For us, a medical mission might have meant my husband kept

busy while I played mom to three confused, bored kids. I can do that at home without typhoid shots and support raising.

You do not want the kids sidelined, especially since, if they are, at least one parent will be, too. Agency experts recommend trips that involve ministering to children with children. That's why going to an orphanage jumped out as a perfect first trip. Our six-year-old could minister in an orphanage right alongside her dad.

Emily met the three girls on the street outside our hotel. They were thrilled to have an American friend. She was thrilled to be a friend. Despite their halting English, the four girls chattered and sang, jumped rope, and played games for an hour or two. Then the three former strangers ended up eating dinner with us down the street. After dinner, our group always walked to the orphanage for crafts and games with the kids. Emily cheerfully invited the girls and one of their mothers, who had joined them, to come along. As we walked, our team leader explained some important social circumstances to Brent and me.

"They'll walk along, but as soon as they realize where we're going, they won't come in. You'll have to explain to Emily. Orphans are too stigmatized here. They're like the 'unclean,' you could say. To go in would be a great social risk. They'll be polite, but these girls and the mom will never go in the building."

At the gates, the girls stopped. They hesitated, looking confused and nervous. Emily smiled at them and put her arms around their shoulders. The mother nodded. They went in.

I don't know if that night will have any earthshaking effect on how Chinese culture views orphans. I know that for one night, three girls discovered they had a lot more in common with 35 orphans than they thought. They learned they could laugh, play games, and talk with them and find them no different than any friend at school. And it wouldn't have happened had they not been invited by a child.

3) Is it safe? Safe is a relative term. Every family will define it differently. We know all mission work entails some risk. But hey, waking up and walking outside my door entails some risk, too. A family unwilling to accept that this is, after all, a leap of faith might want to reconsider. Still, we don't believe families belong in clearly unsafe areas.

For us, China had no real issues of terrorism, drug violence, or uprising to worry about. Post 9-11, we considered ourselves fortunate to have chosen one of the safest countries, politically, we could have found. However, traffic fatalities, especially for pedestrians, rank among the highest in the world. We hadn't prepared mentally for the safety issues presented to us daily.

Car seats are nonexistent and seat belts in short supply. I learned to sit in the back of the bus or taxi so I did not have to watch the driving. There seems to be but one driving rule in China. Use your horn—constantly. Then do as you like. For another interesting touch, one of our hotels also hosted a business gathering during our stay, at which several ladies of questionable profession gathered in our hall nightly. No, we were not in any immediate danger. Still, these situations posed safety dilemmas we'd never faced at home (not to mention awkward conversations with our kids).

Unlike kidnapping threats, certain daily risks we have to swallow hard and accept. The fact is, you do the same thing at home; you just don't recognize it because it appears normal. Everywhere has some risk. You must decide where you'll fall in the fine balance. For a list of countries the State Department considers truly dangerous and warns Americans against traveling to, see http://travel.state.gov/travel/cis_pa_tw/cis/cis_4965.html.

Though I often use forums such as Trip Advisor and Lonely Planet when I plan a family vacation, I would advise caution when consulting them for a volunteer trip. Remember, their purpose is to promote tourism. Their assumption is often that Americans will be "soft" travelers--needing to be pampered and carefully ushered through another country. When I tried to get honest information regarding safety, I was often warned away from going.

On our last trip to Costa Rica, the regional authority told me quite plainly our destination city was not safe, and we should seriously reconsider. Why? No clear answer. I was told a similar story about taking the countrywide bus system. After arriving anyway (I am stubborn, after all), I found the warnings unwarranted. Never once did I feel unsafe for me or my family. Conclusion--tourism sites will point you toward clean, sanitized, on-the-beaten-track experiences. If you want truth, talk to a local, an expat living there, or a previous visitor, or visit the government website.

The Perfect Fit

What kind of work should you look for? The ages, temperaments, and abilities of your children will all affect this choice. With kids under ten, for instance, a construction project might be asking for trouble. On the other hand, if your kids comply easily and will stay out of danger zones and be happy to run gopher trips, maybe construction would be OK. (By the way—if your kids *do* comply easily—could you send them to my house first?)

An overly sensitive child might struggle with seeing extreme poverty and suffering. Alternatively, though, with the right preparation and debriefing, she may benefit from the experience. She may return home energized to continue caring for others long after the plane touches down and mobilize others to help as well.

Hyperactive kids probably shouldn't be put in situations that would require a lot of waiting, downtime, or quiet. We bucked the odds and took three extremely active kids on a 16-hour plane ride and two eight-hour train rides—and they did beautifully. But when I read about other mission trips that require three-hour prayer services or five-hour church—I would think twice (or three, or four, or ten times) before asking that of them. It would simply set up unhappiness all around. Remember —the novelty of the situation will go far toward making easily-bored kids intrigued—but not too far.

A child who needs order and clarity probably won't enjoy trips too open-ended, where participants make it up as they go along. She's already anxious about a new place and people. No structure may stress her too much. In general, mission agencies recommend an itinerary with little downtime for families. Yes—you need some rest and alone time. But for kids, structure works better.

Are your kids shy, gregarious, self-motivated, needing direction? Take temperaments into account when planning the work. But then—let them surprise you.

I didn't believe one classroom could fit 70 kids in it. So unlike our junior high classes at home! The teacher invited us to sit among the kids, and they eagerly made room for us. (Why was it always the boys who eagerly made room for our curly-haired, bright-eyed 12-year-old?!) After questions and answers, the teacher told them we would sign their English books if they wanted.

What we didn't realize was that, apparently, the Chinese have little concept of waiting in lines. I wasn't prepared to be swarmed on all sides by hand, faces, and pens clamoring for attention. Is this what celebrities feel like? Personal space is also, apparently, a very American idea.

I looked over at little Beth, or at least where she had been, lost now in a sea of dark heads. Beth was only six. Very shy. Easily overwhelmed. Of all our kids, she's the one who absolutely needs order. Worried she would be frightened and panic at the crush around her, I wanted to go rescue her, but I knew I'd never get through the throng.

When the bell rang and we were left alone, there she sat, all gap-toothed smiles, with a pile of trinkets on her desk that the students had given her. "That was fun. Can we do it again?" I shook my head in wonder. You just never know what they can do until you let them do it.

To help you decide, brainstorm a list of possible activities. Orphanage work, VBS, street drama, Sunday schools, working with missionaries' kids, going to schools. Ask missionaries on the field what types of work a family should look for.

List your family giftings. If you've never taken a spiritual gifts inventory, this may be the time. It can help you pinpoint if your family would be good at activities involving encouragement, discipling, service, or perhaps mercy. Spiritual gifts tests for kids can be tough to find. You will find a simple inventory in Appendix A. It's not a definitive test, but it will point you toward individual gifts and preferences. When we did this in a high school Sunday School, some of my own kids' responses surprised me. In turn, seeing the results encouraged and energized them, as they discovered they had personal abilities unique to them.

Determine the special skills of your family. Don't limit yourself to the parents' occupational skills. Does someone have a drama bent, or musical talent, people skills, or ability to work with his hands? Take everyone into account. You may still end up stretching yourselves in activities you are not good at, but an inventory to start with could send you in a helpful direction.

The Perfect Place

Really, after satisfying basic safety issues, the place isn't nearly as important as the work and the agency. We planned to look for something nearby (as in this hemisphere at least!) and affordable for our first trip. China didn't occur to me. I have never wanted to go to China. No prior inclination or logical reasoning argued for China. But that's the best work that best fit our family. That's where God clearly pointed. So China it was.

If you have ties to a certain country or a clear sense of God leading you to a place, by all means head in that direction. But be open to place. Any place God sends you will be the right place.

The Perfect Agency

So, where do you start? You can try several different angles when probing for "your" agency or group. The more lures you cast, the more fish to choose from.

❖If your church or denomination supports particular missionaries, try connecting with one that has a family. See if they have needs you can fill. An established missionary family can be ideal to come alongside and truly learn from while doing.

❖Attend a missions conference. Many large churches have mission expositions where you can pick up information and talk to agency representatives. Face-to-face questions and answers can really speed up the process and give you some clarity on just what you're seeking. Even if you don't find the perfect agency, you'll learn a lot and focus your search.

❖Your church or denomination may send short-term mission teams. Check to see if they accept family groups. The organizers will probably have experience in handling details you will greatly appreciate since your details will be multiplied by the number of family members.

❖Browse the Internet. http://www.missionfinder.org even breaks down its opportunities by different codes, one of which alerts you to family-friendly groups. Or try http://www.shorttermmissions.com.

❖Check mission magazines. They'll sometimes have agencies and their website information.

When you've narrowed your search to a few places, start asking questions. E-mail or call the agency to learn more about their program, organization, and planning. Some questions to ask:

✔ Do they take care of logistics (where you eat, sleep, transportation, etc)? You will have enough confusion adapting, and helping your children adapt, to a strange culture and language without adding the stress of figuring out public transportation or ordering meals in restaurants. If you, in addition to ministry and caring for your children in a foreign culture, will have to worry about a thousand and one other daily incidentals that become major in a strange place, you probably want to pass. Ideally, logistics like these are either completely arranged for you or thoroughly explained.

✔ Do they handle your visas? A good agency will walk first-timers through deadlines and expectations clearly and in a timely manner.

✔ Are there clear pre-trip planning guidelines (what to pack, paperwork, fundraising, etc)?

✔ How structured is the work? The more structured and organized the agency, the easier a first-time family will find the experience. Flexibility in missions is absolutely necessary (and part of the fun). But, if an agency doesn't seem to know when and what it's doing, it may lose track of you, too—an uncomfortable feeling if you happen to be 2500 miles from home.

If there is too much, "Well, you'll be free to do ministry in the afternoons," without definitions of what you'll be doing and where, consider that a very yellow light at least. You know what happens with too much down time at home. Five different people go in five different directions. The point of a family mission is to focus as a unit on ministry—so find an agency that externally forces that focus by keeping you busy. Not crazy at all hours until the kids get sick or cranky busy, but structured, scheduled, well-planned busy.

✔ Will the kids get hands-on experience, not just observation? Mission agencies generally feel families should work closely with another established mission family. A remote area or a place with no other children will leave yours out of ministry. Our "established family" had 35 kids—quite enough to keep ours busy! Essentially, choose a place where your kids will find kids to minister to and learn from.

✔ Will you be involved in daily culture and mission life? Building projects can be great, but you really want your kids to experience interacting with the people and learning about a missionary's daily life. A "project" mission where they interact with team members and few others, while a good work to do, may not fulfill your objectives for going in the first place.

✔ What kind of training and debriefing is involved? Kids (and parents) who know what to expect adapt much better. Also, they better understand the significance of their role in the mission. Given the intense emotional involvement in a short-term mission, some assistance in helping your kids readjust to coming home shows the agency's commitment to making your experience positive.

Does the group offer training books, videos, or sessions? Can they give you names of previous short-termers you can talk to about the trip? In our case, training and debriefing had to be condensed. You can't gather twelve people from around the country for six monthly training sessions like you can a church group. But we did receive lots of support and information beforehand and intense preparation when we arrived.

Finally, don't forget the one essential ingredient for choosing your trip.

"That's it!" I shouted. Fortunately, no one else was home. They already shoot me odd looks when I mumble to myself, let alone shout. After looking at about 46 other choices that popped up in my internet search for short-term missions, I read it. "Team members will spend two weeks in an orphanage caring for children." The perfect choice for a family with three girls who loved kids. So we could spend two weeks in . . . let's see, where did it say? China. Whoa. Way too far. Way too costly. Just not in the plan. But it wouldn't leave my head. OK, God. I'll pray about it. The conversation on my side contained a few doubts.

But Lord, the plane ride would be so long.
And it's so different.

And I've never even wanted to go to China.

And God, we'd have to raise $10,000.

And God—my husband's going to lose his job in a few months. So that money isn't coming from us. Don't forget that little detail.

The conversation on His side was brief.
"Are any of those things too hard for me to handle?"
Um, well, that was kind of a rhetorical question, wasn't it God?

Pray. Every family member should pray for God to reveal the right choice. Will He send a divine email telling you "this is the one"? Not too likely. Truthfully, there may be not one "right" choice for you but several. I believe God cares more that you go for the right reasons and change into the right people than go to one specific, perfect spot. So, don't lose sleep over making sure you choose "the one." Narrow your list within the parameters you've set and the questions you've asked. Pray that God helps you eliminate places that would be *wrong* choices for your family.

Then, you may be left with only one good choice or several. Continue to pray. Listen to *everyone* in the family if they feel they have feedback from God. Something will emerge as the choice you feel most drawn to. And if there seem to be logical obstacles in the way of getting there, remember. Are any of those things too hard for Him to handle?

For a suggested trip planning timeline, see Appendix F.

CHAPTER SIX
CAN'T I JUST HIRE A TELEMARKETER?
(FUND RAISING)

Getting shots, eating strange food, flying 16 hours—nothing, *nothing* in all that frightened me so much about going to China as that two-word terror–fund raising. Did I mention I'm an off-the-charts introvert? Did I mention I hate to ask anyone for anything? Did I mention that $10,000 is a lot of big bucks, particularly when you bought a house in the last five years, are still paying off college loans, and your spouse suddenly loses his job? All the excuse I have to offer for such insanity is that God *really* wanted us to go.

Fund-raising strategies will differ depending on your destination and group. The easiest option is going with a team from your church. The entire team works together to raise funds, and sometimes, if you're amazingly lucky, the church has a missions budget that pays for the trip. However, an in-church trip may not be feasible for you. Many churches do not accept family groups. Others are far too small to form a team. You may very likely be looking outside your church at other agencies to spearhead your trip. Because of this, the entire fundraising challenge will fall on you alone. But don't do it alone.

And it *is* a challenge, because you're raising funds not for one person's mission but for an entire family—be it three or ten. The costs for children will likely be less, but not a lot less. They still need visas, eat food, and take up airplane seats. Sometimes, too, others feel less inclined to give to support a six-year-old, reasoning that her "kingdom impact" can't be such a great return on an investment. Of course, they don't realize that the long-term investment in that six-year-old may be compounded astronomically.

Set the Budget

Your agency will generally set the fee for participation. Make sure you know what this includes—taxes, meals, gratuities, etc. You don't want any nasty surprises when the kids demand lunch in New Delhi, it wasn't included, and somehow you don't think the sidewalk vendor's going to run your debit card through a little machine and call it good.

After you have this base amount, factor in other costs not covered. Big ones will include passports and immunizations, often not covered by insurance since these are "elective." Other hidden costs include any supplies you may have to buy (for instance, we each had to bring one craft project to do at the orphanage), gifts for hosts, tips, language books, and travel insurance. Of course, these personal costs cannot be paid by donations to the mission agency—that is solely for your support. But you may be able to set up a separate fund at your church for such personal support. If the check is made out to you, however, the donor may not deduct it from taxes. A sample budget is in Appendix E.

Choose Your Weapon

It is spiritual warfare, after all. Do you think the powers of darkness *want* you to take your family on this experience? Most people find fund raising the place they feel like throwing up their hands and quitting. (For some of us, we actually feel like throwing up *in* our hands. That's how scary it is.) If you get past this—you're almost at the airport you're so close. So, choose carefully.

LETTERS

"I don't know, hon, if we should write to them."

"Why not?"

"Well, for one thing, they're Jewish. How likely are they to support a Christian mission trip? And, she's my doctor as well as your colleague. It feels funny. What if they're offended?"

But I knew we couldn't be too choosy—10,000 dollars is 10,000 dollars, after all. We sent the letter. They sent $500 with a note—"What an exciting opportunity! We hope you and China both gain from this great experience." You just never know, do you?

The most common method of mission fund raising is the letter. You'd be amazed at how many people respond favorably to a simple prayer/fund-raising letter. Just be prepared to keep *very* good records. This, I must tell you, is not my strong point.

While putting my husband through medical school, I once worked in a law office that required a daily balancing of the books. Despite an A in high school calculus, never could I get the simple arithmetic to work out at the end of the day. Lawyers tend to get picky about things like keeping their accounts legal.

As a writer, I've been known to forget where (or when) I sent a certain manuscript out. I've sent the same one to the same editor twice. I've lost entire research folders. The point here—it's a good thing I became a writer instead of a CPA. No, actually, the real point is—if *I* can keep careful records of donations, you can too. So, organize.

First, create a mailing list. Make it as broad as you can imagine. Include family, friends, neighbors, coworkers, church members. Don't be afraid that "so-and-so" may take offense. A low-pressure letter isn't likely to offend. Most people feel pleased you included them and happy to do what they can. We devised different letters for different audiences. A letter to church members may focus more on the spiritual side of missions, while the one to my husband's colleagues talked about the medical conditions and humanitarian assistance we hoped to bring. In writing your support letter, remember a few strategies. (A sample support letter appears in Appendix I.)

➢ Keep it short. A page works well. People like white space, so break up the paragraphs for easy reading.

➢ Add pictures, bullet points, design elements—anything eye-catching but not schlocky. (Are these bullet points schlocky? I hope not.)

➢ Use a font that's easy to read.

➢ Write stories. Facts and statistics are great in moderation, but your supporters want to hear about the individuals you'll be reaching and how you'll help. They want faces and names so they feel they've supported real people with real needs.

- ➢ Explain the monetary cost clearly and without apology. Ask if they can donate X amount so they have a figure in their heads they don't have to come up with. You're giving them the privilege of partnership, not asking for handouts.
- ➢ Let the kids say a few words. Sometimes their enthusiasm stirs more hearts than yours can.
- ➢ Make it easy to contribute with clear instructions and a self-addressed envelope or, best option, a website where they can donate online.
- ➢ Thank them sincerely.

For instance, today I might open my letter with a story like this:

> "Yesterday, I registered my kids for spring classes in gymnastics and art. No one asked about their past, parentage, or papers. I just did it—and I could afford to buy the leotards and art supplies, too.
>
> In six months, we plan to visit children in China for whom life is very different. They are all orphans, abandoned because of deformity, second marriages, death, or poverty. In China, they usually can't go to school. They are taunted by other children and shunned by adults. In Chinese culture, they are unclean—bad luck socially and nonexistent governmentally. They can't ever become other than poor and hopeless. Unless they find an orphanage like the one we're going to work in."

Might that get a potential donor to read on?

We also solicited area churches and service groups. Because we live in a multicultural area, we could target several Chinese churches we hoped would have interest in our mission. I also went to the community women's group of which I was a member. While a secular group that would not normally contribute to a mission per se, they enthusiastically agreed to help because 1) I was one of their own and 2) our goal of serving an orphanage coincided with their goal of serving women and children. So, don't discount secular avenues right away. Find organizations in your area that focus on things you will also focus on, whether that be hunger, girls' education, or any of the countless possibilities. Show up to support and promote an event of theirs, and maybe you can partner together.

An important ingredient for success in these "cold call" situations, however, is follow-up. Friends or family don't usually have to be asked twice, but a letter to another church, service organization, or business should be followed with a phone call or visit for results.

Keep your records well organized so you can be accountable to your donors. Be sure to record all amounts given, by whom, and when. You can do this easily if you already created your master address lists electronically. Mail any checks to your agency promptly, so the donor isn't waiting for weeks for the check to clear. (And so, if you're like me, the check doesn't get buried on the kitchen counter beneath yesterday's school lunch, last week's bills, homework, and the groceries that never got put away.) Most importantly, dispatch a thank-you note promptly, letting them know how deeply you appreciate being entrusted with their investment.

INTERNET

Facebook fundraising works! If every member of your family received even a small donation from every friend on her Facebook list—I'm betting that's a good base right there. Some members of my daughter's current mission team are asking their friends for just $2 or $3 each toward their continuing work. And it works. Don't just send out a request on a status update, though. You know what happens. People read it, think, "how cool is that," and completely forget about it.

Instead, create an event you invite people to. It's a win-win. They feel special to be "part of the group," they have to respond, and you issue a clear time limit and goal.

EVENTS

Fund-raising events are generally the other tool in your support arsenal. The only limits on possibilities lie in your creativity and time. If your church cannot send you as part of a mission team, they can get behind you in support events. For any event, some basic preparation guidelines help.

First, whether you'll be taking a special offering in church or making a presentation before a service organization, practice telling your story and "making a pitch" until you can do it with ease and with a minimum of notes. An audience responds to your eye contact much, much better than to you reading off a prepared speech.

Grab people's attention with an opening story or startling statistic about the people you plan to serve. You have about 30 seconds to make people want to listen—so make sure the first thing you give them is a great hook, not a boring introduction. (Hi. I'm Joe Snead. I want to go to Zimbabwe. That's in Africa. Can you help me?)

Try something more like–"Yesterday, I plunked four quarters in the machine at the mall and got a bottle of the best spring water in Wisconsin. At the same time in Zimbabwe, Nyasha walked 10 miles to the nearest water hole to carry back enough water for her family to live for the day. The hole was almost dry. Four people in her village die every month for lack of clean water. The life expectancy for the entire country is only 35. My family wants to do something about that, and we know you do, too."

In five or ten minutes, be able to tell the story of where you're going and why, what you hope to accomplish, and how these people can help. People give to things that feel personal and immediate. They want to see the individuals you'll see and know exactly what that money will do. Tell them stories of those people, and give specific examples of how you will use their support. Check with the agency you've signed on with to see if they have images or even a prepared powerpoint or video presentation you can use.

Second, be prepared to answer questions. The more knowledgeable you sound, the more worthy of their trust you appear.

Third, stay organized. Communication with the place you'll be making your presentation will be crucial. Know what equipment they have, communicate clearly what you need, determine exactly what they want, for how long, who will be in charge of what, and if they will have an area for you to place pamphlets, letters, displays, and contribution envelopes.

Fourth, start early. Not so early that your supporters may get the letter and think, "Oh, we've got nine months to get them a check," but early enough to plan an organized campaign and pull off as many events as you may need without crowding them together, creating overkill with your support base, and exhausting you before you even leave.

Ideas for fund-raising events:

☆ a special offering in church on Sunday morning

☆ a churchwide yard sale. Get involvement from as many friends and neighbors as you can. Advertise *why* you're holding the sale, if you have access to free advertisements. We had a lot of success this last trip with haivng a "dollar sale." Everything there was $1. No kidding. It seems counterintuitive, but believe we raised more money than we would have otherwise.

☆ a silent auction. Members of the congregation or area businesses can donate items for which others will bid.

☆ bake sales. An interesting twist would be to have a bake off sale. Invite people to compete for the top baking honors, and sell the treats that pour in.

☆ sports tournaments. Teams or individuals pay entry fees to compete in 3-on-3 basketball, soccer, volleyball, tennis, bean bag toss, or hey, even mini-golf. (At least most of us wouldn't hurt ourselves on that one.)

☆ "Thons". Choose something your family or group likes to do and take pledges to do that--for a very, very long time! Twenty-four hours of charades, anyone?

☆ a specialty dinner. Offer an international meal, a special holiday feast, or a mystery dinner.

☆ contests: talents, cooking, etc. Entrants pay a fee, as do attendees.

☆ a pancake breakfast

☆ scavenger hunt. Teams pay to enter, and the winning team gets dinner. (You can do this in conjunction with the international meal above.)

☆ Offer your services for a monthly treat. We've taken bids for pie-of-the-month, something I'd definitely buy into! What do family members enjoy doing? Baking, cooking an international meal, washing cars, personal shopping? Someone might want that service once a month until you leave for your trip.

☆ buying shares. Determine how much money would buy a bag of cement for your building project or VBS books for the orphanage. Then "sell" the "shares" to people and give them their share certificates. It's kind of like putting their names on a brick—something tangible a donor can look at and say, "I did that!"

☆ pastor's pledge. Get your pastor to promise something outlandish if the church gives X amount. One pastor preached from the church rooftop on this one. Our Community Life pastor recently submitted to a mohawk when our daughter successfully raised her support for three months in Guatemala.

☆ Plant sale. I almost guarantee some people in your church love to garden and also love to share what they've grown. Have a spring or fall plant sale using what they get out of their yards. You could add to it with homemade jams, vinegars, crafts, etc. out of the garden.

☆ Yard clean up. Offer church members' services in the community to do spring or fall cleanup. Another option could be taking down/putting up Christmas lights, a chore most people would gladly donate for someone else to do!

☆ Make a google search for creative fundraising that works for you. Try www.fundraiserinsight.-org/ideas as one great resource.

Remember in all this—the apostle Paul didn't shrink from telling others of his needs in order to continue his short-term mission trips. He shared honestly and completely how others could, and should, help. He told the stories of those to whom he ministered. Paul knew the truth—he wasn't soliciting or selling anything. He was offering people a chance to change someone else's life. Not surprisingly, most people appreciated the chance.

CHAPTER SEVEN
PASSPORTS AND SHOTS AND PACKING—OH MY!
(PHYSICAL PREPARATION)

Passports

Getting passports proved traumatic. Well, not *getting* passports, actually. The trauma occurred when I pulled out my old passport from high school and the kids insisted on seeing the picture. I didn't consider hysterical laughter the appropriate response. I mean, Farrah hair was very in when I was 16, and I did it well, I must say. They only rolled their eyes and thanked Jesus they hadn't lived in the late 70s.

The passport process isn't particularly painful, but as with all things governmental, it must be done precisely and with plenty of lead time. Currently, passport cards suffice for Canada, Mexico, the Caribbean, and the Bahamas, a cheaper alternative to a full passport *if* you are traveling by land or sea (**not** by air). But rules change—keep abreast.

Give yourselves a few months to complete the application process. Expedited passports are possible, but they will cost you $60 *each* in addition to the normal fee. So apply early!

To apply for passports you'll need:

- ✓ A certified copy of *every* family member's birth certificate. You cannot use a photocopy, hospital copy, or notarized copy. You must obtain an official certificate with embossed seal from the state of birth.

- ✓ If you have an expired passport, as I did, you can use it as acceptable proof of birth.

- ✓ Two passport photos. These cannot be your own snapshots. They must meet certain specifications of size and facial view. Any one-hour photo center usually takes passport photos exactly as the government wants them. (We had ours done at Walgreens.)

- ✓ The passport application. You can obtain these online at www.state.gov or at an application center. The website will also give you information on the passport application center nearest to your zip code—usually found in county offices and even some post offices and colleges.

- ✓ Money. Passports aren't cheap—especially if you multiply the cost for every family member. Be prepared to pay for this upfront, as it isn't included in your support fee. Current fees (as of 2013) are $165 for first-time adults and $120 for children under 16.

"Is that a real gun?" whispered Emily. Becca considered a remark on how like terrorists we all looked and, fortunately, thought better of it. Beth just stared with wide eyes and shrunk behind me. Entering the county court building surrounded by armed guards spooked the kids a bit, let's just say. But with

everything in order, it didn't take too long to compete the process. Later, as we left the office, the older two girls complained about their horribly embarrassing passport photos. Someday, their kids will get a good laugh at them. Life is fair, after all.

Visas

An established agency will probably take care of visa arrangements. If you're going on your own, this will be your job. Some countries will not require visas to enter, but others will. The same government web site (http://travel.state.gov/visa/visa_1750.html) contains consular information sheets (under travel warnings) which will explain each country's entry requirements.

In filling out the visa application, take special care when listing your profession and the reason for entering the country. A "closed" or "sensitive" to the gospel country (such as two I've entered on mission trips—China and East Germany) will do more than look askance at "Christian mission work" on your application. Not only would you be denied entry should you mention a Christian activity or profession, but you could compromise the entire team as well as national contacts within the country.

Instead, you could enter tourism as your reason—you will be seeing the sights, won't you? And if you are a pastor or other ministry professional, perhaps "speaker" or "counselor" might be a better job title to list.

Parent Authorization

If one parent travels alone with a child, take note at state.gov as well to see if you will be required to present proof that the absent parent has given permission to travel. Many countries, sensitive to parental abduction of minors, require *notarized* proof that one parent signed an agreement allowing the other to take the child of the country. To be safe, assume you will need this. Better to obtain such a letter and not need it than not to have it and be denied entry at the arrival airport. A sample form appears in Appendix D.

In general, the state.gov site offers a treasure trove of helpful tips and answers for families abroad. Click on "travel and business" to find:

▶Updated lists of what is and is not permissible in carry-on luggage. These rules have changed twice in the last month or two. You can see, it's helpful to stay current. You don't want to waste precious time at checkpoints because you tried to carry on gel shoe inserts or unmarked prescription drugs. They even have helpful cards to print out with clear information and directions.

▶Current travel warnings. These contain countries Americans are cautioned to avoid.

▶Advice for traveling with babies or special medical needs.

▶What to expect at airports, checkpoints, customs, etc.

▶Current security levels.

▶Consular information sheets offering publications such as "A Safe Trip Abroad" and "Passports the Easy Way."

▶"Countries and Regions" gives background information, contacts for more information, and embassy websites and e-mails.

▶Per diem rates.

▶A site for finding the nearest passport facility by plugging in your zip code.

When the new passports arrived, the Farrah-do had given way to middle-age curly bob, and the 70's to the 2000's with my new passport. I hoped it would get a lot of use. And proper respect for the new photo.

Health Issues

"Shots?! You didn't say anything about getting *shots* to go to China!" Suddenly, the kids weren't so sure. Fortunately, three things helped ease their medical worries:

One—They really wanted to go, and thus considered it worth the supreme sacrifice of allowing needles within 100 feet of their skinny little arms. Two—they talked to their cousin Hannah who has lived abroad in various countries all her life and believes herself an expert at "shots of the world." Three—they discovered mom had to get more shots than they did. And they got to watch.

Immunization requirements vary by country. If a destination country does not require any, public health officials still may recommend some. We had no required shots for China, but conversation with an international health nurse strongly suggested typhoid (an oral vaccine), hepatitis, and polio for those who hadn't received a live virus.

Again, the consular information sheets will have helpful information on the subject. Shots or medicines (like those for typhoid, malaria, and hepatitis), may come in a series, too, so ask a health care professional about that possibility, and give yourself time to get them all in before departure.

It's a good idea to find a medical professional in your area with whom you can discuss health precautions. We have a university facility nearby, so we easily found an international health practitioner. Not only could we get advice for immunizations, but we received suggestions for foods to avoid, sanitary procedures, and general health safety. The Centers for Disease Control's website (http://www.cdc.gov) has a link for "travel medicine clinics" to help you find a professional near you.

Traveling with children presents special health risks. Because of their smaller size, less developed immune systems, and less than careful habits, children can be more susceptible to disease and its effects than adults. The three most common dangers for children traveling abroad, according to the CDC, are diarrhea, motor vehicle accidents, and drowning. To safeguard yourself from medical inconvenience or disaster, educate your kids and follow some basic precautions.

—Make sure your children thoroughly understand the health issues and precautions. For instance, our physician cautioned us not to eat milk products. The girls dutifully drank soy milk and avoided cheese for two weeks. But—on the last night, one of them happily accepted an ice cream cone bought by another team member. She didn't connect "milk" with "ice cream." (Possibly a case of wishful thinking?)

Make sure you completely define terms like "dairy products" and "raw vegetables." Absolutely define "water." Kids will readily understand not to drink a glass of water from a tap or fountain. But—will they realize that includes ice cubes? Drinks mixed with water such as lemonade? Brushing their teeth with tap water? Ingesting any amount of water in the bath or shower?

—Make sure kids take, but not overtake, malarial medication. Be sure they continue for as long *before and after* the trip as your doctor has prescribed.

—Bring hand sanitizer and use it. Use it before eating, after peeling fruit, going to the bathroom, or having a lot of contact with other people. But be discreet—don't make a production of washing after you shake your host's hand!

—Avoid all unbottled water. Drink only bottled water, canned or bottled soft drinks, or boiled water drinks. Check the seals on your water bottles. Our leader in China told us that some vendors refilled used bottles with tap water.

—Avoid unpeeled, raw fruit and vegetables. They could have been washed in contaminated water. Peel them yourself, then eat them.

—Avoid undercooked or uncooked meat.

—Avoid street vendor foods.

—Keep a sharper eye than usual on kids. They are not used to having to be careful about everything they touch or eat. They are not naturally all that cautious. They will need your eyes and ears to keep them alert.

—Have a thorough check-up before going to uncover any potential problems that could arise while overseas. The middle of Mozambique is *not* the place to discover you have a heart condition.

—Know how to contact your insurance carrier. Find out if they cover medical evacuation to a first-world hospital in case of emergency. If not (and probably not), you should strongly consider adding this kind of coverage while you are gone. You do not want a medical emergency overseas and only then discover your two options: 1) accept treatment at a local hospital which may not have adequate knowledge, equipment, or sanitation; or 2) shoulder the enormous cost of an emergency air ride home yourself. Insurance companies have riders you can add for such emergency situations.

Packing

Daniel bought Beth the little Chinese hat at a vendor booth near the Great Wall. She wore it everywhere. Long brown hair streaming from under the cone of straw, she walked ahead of us, pulling her blue Pooh Bear suitcase on wheels. Thank goodness for the Pooh Bear suitcase. We had to tote our luggage everywhere — airport to buses to hotels to train stations to ministry sites — and most of these were not close together.

Well behind our six-year-old, one of the other team members trudged along with her two enormous suitcases. "Why, she grumbled for the fifth time, did I pack a hair dryer?!"

The best packing advice I can offer—when the sending agency says "pack light"—pay attention! The last thing you want when you travel dusty, questionable roads or traverse huge train stations is tired, cranky kids who don't want to carry their belongings one more step. The second-to-last thing you don't want is to have to carry the things yourself—because then you'll be the tired, cranky one.

"One pair of shoes? Are you serious?" our oldest squealed. "And those shoes—mom." She eyed the chunky Land's End slip-ons I had purchased for their ruggedness and comfort, not style. "They're soooo ugly."

"Yeah, maybe. But you'll be walking a lot and you need sturdy shoes. And you don't need to carry extra ones. Just trust me."

"Sure. Right." Barely audible grumbling followed her out of the rom. Becca had never been big on the 'just trust me' line.

By the end of two weeks, no one would have recognized the shoes. Formerly lavender suede, now they sported some muddy-dusty-purply undefinable hue. Still as tough and comfy as ever, though. Plus, we had one preteen very happy she hadn't ruined any of her more fashionable footwear. Or carried it.

"Are you glad we got the shoes?"
*"I'm glad I **had** them. But I don't ever have to wear them again, do I? In public?"*

Limit each family member to one small case and possibly a backpack. Invest in luggage with wheels—definitely! You *will* be toting it around. I can't stress this enough—don't overload with more than each person can comfortably carry him or herself. So, people, you really don't need:

◘ That hair dryer. It won't work anyway without an adapter, which adds more luggage. If you have electricity at all. In fact, just about any electrical gadget could be left at home because: one, it might not work; two, you won't have time to use it; and three, you don't need it.

◘ Make up. Same story. You're not likely to have a fancy night out, and you won't have time to bother with it. Additionally, Christians in some cultures may be disturbed by women in make up. (OK, they'd be even more disturbed by men in make up.) For them, it may be a sign of worldliness or even loose morals. This is not a cultural stumbling block you need to erect. Yes—I know. Tell that to your teenage daughter who can't leave her bedroom without lip gloss.

◘ Credit cards and unnecessary identification. It only leaves you more vulnerable to theft. Take a driver's license, one or two credit cards, and your passport. Leave everything else home.

◘ Expensive camera equipment. Again, this makes you a theft target. It also tends to divert you from your reason for being there if you are a photoholic (which, of course, you are if you have expensive equipment). A simple camera for memories works great. As a plus, bring some photos of your family to give to people you meet. We brought a pocket Polaroid-type camera that takes small wallet-sized pictures. It was the hit of the week. Every child we met in China wanted a picture of himself with our kids, and they got one with that camera.

◘ Clothing and jewelry that looks expensive or flashy. Basically, avoid the appearance of "affluent Americans." Not only could it prove dangerous to you, but it could put obstacles in the way of your relating to the people.

◘ Electronics equipment. Just why would you need an iPad or iPod? See above about "affluence."

◘ Evangelical literature, Bibles, or religious material of any kind if you're crossing into a closed or sensitive country. One Bible for personal use usually doesn't cause trouble, but if it looks like you plan to leave any Christian materials there, you may be denied entry at the border. Heed the dictates of your agency carefully. Do *not* try to play Lone Ranger Bible smuggler. This isn't the movies, and these are real peoples' lives.

So What *Should* You Bring?

I stood in front of the stall doors at the Great Wall of China official bathroom. Three little hands waved over the tops of the doors, searching for the tissues I held. Of course, I had to snap a picture of the frantic waving hands before I dug into my purse. After all, it was all part of the experience that I should document, right?

"Mom, come on!"
"Really, you're a little impatient," I teased.
"We'll have to do this for two whole weeks?" they whined.
"Oh, it will be much worse than this." The voice came from another stall, that of a seasoned team member.

"Welcome to your first cross-cultural experience," I said, laughing. "Now let me in for my turn. But — I keep the tissue pack."

Yes, there are some things you definitely *should* bring to a foreign country. You'll find a sample packing list in Appendix C.

- A money belt. You can find these at travel or luggage stores or online. Worn under your clothes and close to your body, they are the safest way to carry your money and passports. If you carry the family passports in your purse thrown over your shoulder and it gets snagged by someone in a passing car, what are you going to do?

- A list of sponsors, friends, and relatives to send postcards or e-mail. If you're really efficient, you can address postcards before you leave.

- Small packets of tissues. It's a lot more compact than a roll of toilet paper in a suitcase (and a lot more portable and less embarrassing to carry!). Trust me — you *do not* want to assume toilet paper is a staple in the country you choose. Carry a tissue packet everywhere.

- Basic first aid needs. Sunscreen, insect repellent, acetaminophen, anti-diarrheal medication, and medication for indigestion, Band-Aids, antiseptic, and hydrocortisone cream. For sensitive systems that an unusual diet may upset, fiber pills help a lot, too. Don't forget the lip balm and maybe saline spray for dryer climates.

◘ Any prescription medicines should stay in the original containers and be put in carry-on luggage. Bring copies of your prescriptions.

◘ Travel-size sample bottles of shampoo, body wash, laundry detergent, etc. zipped up in a sealed plastic bag. Leaks in your luggage ruin an excited arrival.

◘ Casual, modest, wrinkle-proof, durable clothing that mixes and matches well. Ladies — some cultures will expect skirts, and almost all will expect more modesty in attire than you're used to here. Better safe than an embarrassment to the ministry. Leave the short shorts and spaghetti straps at home.

◘ A spare pair of glasses. I've always scoffed at this one. Until last December when my only glasses got lost on the plane, along with the extra pair of contacts I had put in the case. It was *not* a good two weeks, visually.

◘ A foldable bag for any purchases you make in the country. It goes over folded neatly in your suitcase, returns full in checked baggage.

◘ The smallest foldable umbrella you can find.

◘ A journal. You'll have so many impressions, conversations, and memories you want to keep, and they will get all jumbled up in your memory unless you write them down. You definitely won't want to lose them. Also, a journal makes it easier later to report on your trip. Let all family members contribute their thoughts or drawings to make a real family keepsake. Pack extra pens. Consider a small digital recorder.

◘ A notebook of phonetic spellings of necessary phrases. *Thank you. Where is the bathroom? Please. You're welcome. We are Christians from America.* Nothing could top the astonishment and shy gratitude of the classroom of kids who asked our daughter why she came all this way to help orphans and talk to them. "Because, "Jesu ai ni"—Jesus loves you," she said. She knew very little more Chinese. She didn't have to.

◘ Spare batteries and memory card for the camera.

◘ One pair of sturdy working\walking shoes and one pair of slip-on sandal type shoes.

◘ Work clothes and gloves if you need these items.

◘ A battery-operated alarm clock if you can't use your phone.

◘ Helpful items might also include a small sewing kit and a retractable travel clothesline (you *will* be handwashing). We have photos of underwear drying all over lamps and chairs in a hotel room in China. You can avoid those embarrassing photos with that clothesline.

◘ Possibly, depending on where you will stay: a towel, washcloth, bathrobe, and modest swimwear.

◘ Your drivers license, the credit card you may use, and a photocopy of your passports and airline tickets. Leave a copy of all these at home with a friend, as well.

◘ Photos of your family and small gifts for your hosts.

Getting documents, shots, and supplies gets you physically prepared for your trip. The real preparation, though, takes place in less tangible areas. The best item you can bring with you can't be packed neatly in a suitcase. But it will prove to be the most important gift you could give to your host and the people you serve. Unfortunately, you can't pack "Ten Easy Ways to Understand a Culture" or get immunized for costly social error. For this, you need a different kind of preparation.

CHAPTER EIGHT
DON'T EVER CROSS THE CHOPSTICKS
(EDUCATIONAL PREPARATION)

"Packing light" doesn't apply only to clothing and hair dryers. When entering into a cross-cultural experience, we need to jettison a lot of other baggage as well.

In general, Americans make assumptions that others just don't view as the "givens" we believe them to be. Assumptions about time, freedom, individualism, privacy, family, hygiene—what we take for granted actually can seem rather odd to most of the rest of the world. And as privileged visitors in their world, it is we who must bend.

"Mom, they're all watching me!" Our daughter's whispered squeal came from somewhere about three stalls down in the junior high ladies' room.

"Um, yeah. Me, too, sweetheart. Just, ah, try to pretend they're not there?"

A lot easier said than done, given that the doorless white cinder-block stalls offered plenty of viewing area to the curious public. Not only had the dozen girls and female teachers politely shown us to the bathroom, they had gone in with us, presumably to see for themselves if white women did their business any differently than they. I half-expected to see score cards flashing up with our rating on squatty-potty proficiency.

In a country with one and a half billion people, the vast majority of whom live on the eastern third of the land, people don't prize privacy as we do in America. They can't. With a touch of claustrophobia, I struggled to adapt to city streets, parks, and playgrounds where people pressed together like children around a piñata. When classroom teachers told their students (70 or 80 in a room) they could get the Americans to autograph their English books, I expected orderly lines of children. I got a crushing mass of hands and pens, which I assumed were attached to faces I couldn't see in the chaos.

Everywhere, curious people wanted to see, talk to, and touch the strangers. As a family of introverts for whom "personal space" is a necessity for mental health, we found its nonexistence in Chinese culture challenging. Apparently, mission organizers recognized this likelihood for Americans and built in some down time to allow us to retreat behind hotel room doors. Not a lot, but some.

What should you do when culture shock shocks you? First of all—rejoice! Yep, that's right. The fact that you are shocked means you're doing more than just gliding through the country like a tourist, all surface, no content. It means you're actively engaging—and that's a good thing. Then, try to pinpoint exactly what "excess baggage" you're carrying around. What about the situation discomfits you? What assumptions do you bring to the situation that may not fit the culture you've entered?

Often, our inappropriate assumptions fall into one of two categories. First, our certainty that we know the way things *should* be interferes with our understanding of the way things *are*. Second, our convictions about why we've come keep us from deeper interaction.

The slab of cardboard halfway in the street shifted as our bus approached it. Then, we all realized why. A foot protruded beneath the brown rectangle, begging, it seemed, for someone to run it over. With united horror, team members on the bus protested to stop and help the homeless man to safety out of the street and a good meal. But the experienced leaders shook their heads. "We can't. It would do more harm than good. Trust us. I know it seems wrong to you. But we know how this culture works."

It wasn't our first or last struggle in integrating how things "should" be with reality. Of course, God has a way all things should be. But are you really sure you know exactly what it us? Even if you are, do you know exactly how to implement it in any situation and any culture? You might be surprised to realize how many of our "shoulds" are far more North American culture-based than Bible mandated.

Whenever you catch yourself thinking "but these people should . . ." send that thought firmly back home without a passport. Then start opening your mind with questions rather than statements. Why do they do this? How do they tackle this issue? What in their background makes them respond this way? Most people don't get offended by honest, non-accusing questions. They feel pleased you want to learn from them. (Not surprisingly, this non-judgmental approach works well with Americans as well!)

"Have you been anywhere else in Asia?" The teacher we met at the teahouse eagerly practiced her English with us in polite conversation. She held herself back somewhat, a little reticent with strangers but full of intelligent, insightful questions.

"Well, we spent a few days in Beijing," we began. "And stopped in Tokyo to change planes, if that counts as visiting Japan."

Behind the tortoise shell glasses her eyes hardened. "I hate the Japanese. You should never go there."

"Oh. I'm sorry. Why?"

"Because of what they did. They killed millions of Chinese. During the war. They are evil."

"But, but," I stammered. "That was sixty years ago. Most of the people who did that are dead now."

"It doesn't matter. All Japanese are evil. I hate them."

We could have ended that conversation quickly with an admonition that we should not hate anyone. Told her that her hostility was irrational. But we were not in that teashop to change her moral values but to point her toward the One who could. To do that, we had to understand the ultimate concepts behind her hatred and the whys of its existence.

Our pre-trip study of the "religion" of communism (and the Buddhism which proceeded it) helped us realize the primary deficiency behind the labyrinth of loathing she'd erected. Grace. *Nothing* in her education or cultural background taught her the concept of forgiving one's enemies or offering a sacrifice for the undeserving.

How could we presume to tell her how the pieces of her puzzle should fit when she didn't have the framework to put them in? She didn't even have the picture on the front of the box. So instead, we told her a story of grace. A story of a righteous judge who sentences a man to death —the just penalty for his crimes. Then, he allows his own son to take the man's punishment.

"I do not understand this thought," she responded. Her puzzled eyes declared her honesty. She really didn't. She couldn't. But she was, for the first time in her loyal communist life, intrigued. She agreed to read more about this Jesus. And, for the first time, I truly understood what it would be like to live without the grace of Jesus.

It's kind of like admonishing Ehud Olmert and Mahmoud Abbas to "shake hands and play nice." Yeah, we'll see how well that works out. We can't expect a person to live by Christian principles if his frame of reference doesn't include Christian teaching. Honestly, it's hard enough for those of us who *do* have the puzzle frame.

And, there are plenty of things in our culture that Christians from other lands look at askance—with good reason. How much of our North American Christianity do we assume is from the Bible when it's really for our culture? How much of our culture could a believer from, say, Malawi, judge just as much we as judge others?

Deal with grace with what is; give up your assumptions about what should be, and your culture shock will be less shocking.

Because they have less experience with the ways of reality, children tend to expect the world to reflect their ideals more than adults do. They simply perceive the world through a much more black and white viewfinder. Because of this, kids will experience greater conflict of expectations vs. reality than their parents.

Let them. Our kids can usually wrestle with tougher things than we think. Let them ask questions. Don't be afraid to say, "I don't know" or to show your emotions on the subject. Help them to realize the difference between "different" and "wrong." The first carries no moral judgment. Learning the difference teaches your kids tolerance, grace, and adaptability.

Most things you struggle with will fall into the "different" category. And the truly wrong you cannot right in two weeks' time. But your children will grow up more aware of societal injustice and less willing to stand on the sidelines when they do have the opportunity to affect change.

Our other troublesome assumptions center around the question—why are we here? The altruism that spurs most families to missions springs from wonderful motives. Yet North American altruism tends to be very goal oriented —"We'll fix the problem; we'll teach you the *right* way." With the best of intentions, you may be perceived as trying to "fix" their culture rather than working with them toward mutual benefit.

Unlike the first issue, on this one kids have the advantage over their parents. Perhaps it's because they spend most of their days learning rather than teaching. Maybe they focus more energy on growing than managing. Or their natural curiosity and willingness to make friends helps them. Whatever the reason, adults tend to approach a culture thinking "I'm going to teach them," while kids often think, "I'm going to learn about them." Guess which approach opens more doors?

Unable to openly speak of Jesus or God's love to the orphans, the adults on our team struggled with questions of how to convey the message we couldn't share audibly. Our three kids, meanwhile, played with them, learned songs from them, hugged them, and became friends.

Chinese culture shuns orphans. Other children do not play with or hug them. But these three did. And not just any three—three American children, practically gods from another planet as far as they were concerned. It would be like Justin Bieber dropping by your daughter's slumber party and joining in the games. And the message got through. *People who believe in Jesus treat us like we've always dreamed of being treated.* Who really needed words, after all?

Why are you there? To impart your great knowledge and compassion? Or to treat them like Jesus would—with respect and love? Teaching is great—but being taught may be more valuable. Answering questions is marvelous—but just maybe, ask more than you answer.

Learning Before You Go

As a writer, I need to do my research. If I planned to interview Lovie Smith, I'd better know he took his team to the Superbowl in '07 for the first time in twenty-one years. (And believe me, as a lifelong Bears fan, I know.) If I plan to talk to J.K. Rowling, I ought to pick up a couple of her books. If I want to set a novel in Seattle in 1810, well, I'd better plan to use Duwamish Indians for characters, not white settlers. If you want to connect with people in another country, you need to do research, too. Learning before you go helps your transition into another culture and tells the people there, "I'm interested. You're valuable to me."

Coincidentally, the year we went to China we also decided to homeschool our oldest daughter for sixth grade. Guess what she studied for the first month of school? By October, Becca could give us all a brief history of China, an in-depth analysis of the Cultural Revolution, and an overview of its geography, economy, and national landmarks. She could (and did) even cook an authentic meal.

Before you go, spend some time together learning about your destination country. You can approach this in a variety of ways, but make it fun rather than feeling too much like school work.

—Try assigning each family member a topic to research. Ideas could include geography, politics, history, current events, language, customs, holidays, or religion. Make a game of each person coming to the dinner table with a trivia question or a "did you know?" fact. (Did you know the roofs in the Forbidden Palace are yellow? And that there are small statuettes on each corner of the roofs, the number of which designated the power of the person living within the building? Did you know what number was reserved for the emperor?)

—See if you can incorporate learning into a school, scouting, or a 4H project. An English assignment for a persuasive paper could focus on the plight of orphans in China, or soldier boys in Sudan. A citizenship badge could compare two systems of government, ours and theirs.

—Research games played in the country and learn them together.

—Cook dinners together using recipes from the country. (We discovered something funny. We almost never ate in China what Americans consider Chinese food. The cuisine varies enormously between regions, and some of the things we call Chinese aren't Chinese at all!)

—Find CDs or podcasts of basic phrases in the language. Or take a conversational course at a local community college. Meet someone who speaks the language and invite him or her to dinner. Learning even a few phrases helps you feel less uncertain and shows people you respect them. Even Beth learned quickly the

Chinese for basic phrases—Hello, thank you, good bye, I'm fine. Jesus loves you. (Beware of literal translations. We learned there's no real phrase for "you're welcome" in Chinese. If we used the literal words "you're welcome," we'd be inviting people to our home, not responding to "thank you." And someone might well take us up on it!) Many websites and apps offer free language education. One we've used a lot in preparing for Costa Rica is http://www.spanishdict.com, and there are many more out there.

—Cut out current events stories from newspapers and magazines that relate to your country. Make a bulletin board collage of them.

—Read a lot. Not just non-fiction either. Find fiction or biography by native authors or about the country. Reading about the Cultural Revolution wouldn't have had the impact on our daughter that reading *Red Scarf Girl*, the memoir of a girl enduring it, did.

—Celebrate holidays of the country. Learn when they are and how they are celebrated, then have your own family party.

— Play games to learn about cross-cultural experience. http://wilderdom.com/games/MulticulturalExperientialActivities.html offers some great ideas.

—Check guidebooks out of the library. (Easy to find on China. A little tougher, perhaps for, say, Somalia. It only works for some destinations.) You may also find DVDs to watch together.

—If you live near a university, invite an international student into your home. Learning firsthand from a native can't be beat!

—Check travel blogs or talk to veteran travelers you know. Reading others' experiences helps you see what mistakes to avoid and what to ensure you don't miss.

Specific Cultural Issues

My husband handed the taxi driver the card containing our hotel's address in Chinese. The man grinned, nodded, and tore away from the curb before we were quite seated. We enjoyed the lights whizzing by and the excitement of nightlife in Beijing. One street we had walked down more than once beckoned me often with its shooting stars for streetlights and cacophony of colors. The Chinese invented fireworks, and somehow, the streets at night in the city looked as if they used all that imagination to light up the night without need of pyrotechnics. I loved it.

But hadn't we seen those particular lights once before? And wait—I'm quite sure we've never gotten on a freeway to go back to the hotel. Finally, the third time we circled by the miniature Eiffel Tower, we knew something was amiss. I began to panic at the thought that our cabdriver was actually abducting the silly American family who trusted him—and no one would ever know where the bodies turned up.

Our daughter thought perhaps he didn't understand the directions. My husband, sensibly, assumed he was literally taking us for a ride, intending to charge three or four times the amount it should have cost to return to the hotel. Brent started pointing to the card and yelling in English. Our driver shrugged and looked innocent. "We won't pay!" Brent told him, pointing to the meter. That he somehow understood, and within a couple minutes we landed at our destination.

Thus, we learned a bit more than we had wanted about cross-cultural non-communication. Luckily for us, we did not learn about cross-cultural law enforcement, since, if the driver had chosen to call in police, we would surely have been on the losing side of any argument.

Though potential issues vary with your destination, your family may encounter some fairly universal concerns.

Food often brings out the most parental worry. What will we have to eat? Will my kids eat it? This will be more or less of an issue depending on where you go and what arrangements you have. We usually ate in restaurants, and in typical Chinese style, several dishes sat on the central lazy susan. We could opt to try one or all, and no host would be offended. Pretty adventurous eaters, our kids dug in. (We learned the hard way, though what not to put on the lazy susan. An opened can of Sprite makes quite a mess when spun with the vigor of an eleven-year-old.)

The only culinary offering I think the kids would have refused to eat was the fish head. Fortunately, etiquette reserved that delicacy for the eldest at the table. Also fortunately, I missed that designation. We instructed the girls never to ask what they were eating. Just eat it in blissful ignorance.

If you have picky eaters, keep that in mind when choosing a destination and accommodations. Some missions tell you they will be eating in homes or churches —so you'd better be ready to graciously eat whatever they serve. Others make more use of restaurants and communal eating situations—more flexibility for finicky palates. Only you can judge your tolerance levels.

Set a good example yourself of adventurous eating. Recently, my daughter wanted to try sushi—a taste experience I've never had at the top of my "must try" list. But heeding my New Year's resolution to live without fear, I swallowed raw eel and seaweed. Don't think it will ever be a staple of my diet, but at least they all witnessed my willingness to try.

Explain to the kids the importance of not insulting their host. Even young children can understand not hurting another's feelings, and they will feel very "grown up" knowing their reactions really do matter. So no grimmacing, no "what's this?" no "eeew, gross," no questions, no kidding. If you're worried your kids may eat nothing but white rice for two weeks, bring along some healthy snacks, such as dried fruit, nuts, peanut butter crackers, and yogurt covered raisins. (Make sure these items will be allowed past customs.)

Food allergies, of course, present a bigger issue. If your kids have serious allergies, do some research on the food in that country. Know ahead of time what to avoid. Pack extra food for that child, and any needed medical supplies in case something is accidentally eaten that shouldn't be.

Dress could present another sticky issue, especially with teens. Styles of dress in this country, for young women in particular, may be extremely inappropriate in another country. Help your kids understand that you're going as servants to other people, and therefore they may have to sacrifice their concept of "looking good" for the overall good. Leave home the spaghetti straps, mini skirts, bikinis, short shorts, or halter tops. In some countries, girls and women will be expected to wear only skirts and dresses, and only knee-length or below. (I don't know about guys, but I'm guessing the boxers-hanging-out look won't fly too well in some places, either.)

Watch, too, that the style and sheer amount of your clothing doesn't scream "I'm a rich American." You may sport perfectly modest, non-offensive clothing and still create a cultural rift by simply having too much of it, while the people you minister with have only two outfits, total.

Time. Our former pastor (who is black) used to joke about what he called CPT—colored people time. When an event started late or ran way overtime, he said it was operating on CPT. A more fluid definition of punctuality.

In fact, our obsession with punctuality distinctly identifies American culture. Rather than prioritize task and timeline as we do, many other cultures emphasize relationship and process. An American construction team, for instance, might focus entirely on getting a building finished in their two weeks—completing the task. Nationals, however, may prefer to finish one third of the construction and instead build relationships with the team members—an opportunity you will totally miss if you remain task-focused. Repeat after me the missions mantra —*be flexible*.

On our first visit to Costa Rica, the team wanted to begin work immediately--as in the moment we pulled into the hotel. But culturally, we needed to understand the time it would take for the people there to get to know us, trust us, and be willing to show us what we needed to know. Their priority was in discovering whether we were there to create a long-term relationship or to fly in and fly out. It made a huge difference, and it took time.

In time, leaders took us to see the neighborhood they wanted to help and allowed us to hear their dream. But they needed that time, and we needed to give it to them. Now, we have a relationship that will allow us to return and to carry on communication while at home. That would never have happened had we pushed our agenda.

Hygiene. The place you go may or may not have clean water, indoor plumbing, or dental care. The people you meet may or may not have everyday knowledge of deodorant, toothpaste, or razors. You only happen to live in a culture that does. Kids raised in a country where we advertise antibacterial tissues and supply wipes for shopping carts can't anticipate the different levels of hygiene practices they may encounter.

Explain to them *before* they publicly announce that someone "sure has bad BO" that such opinions should not be shared out loud. Children (and adults) should know never to comment on the native peoples' appearance, smell, or habits. (As an fyi, that's generally polite in the US as well!)

Help kids understand that some differences are merely cultural (like women shaving). Others occur because of diet (i,e, breath odors), and still others because adequate health care is unavailable. In any case, the people they meet are God's creatures in His image—and you wouldn't remark to others that Jesus smelled funny, would you? (Hey, by American standards, he almost certainly did!)

Also, make yourself aware of hygiene practices that you must follow in order not to be culturally offensive. For example, if you have a left-handed child and you travel to India, be careful. That hand is "unclean" in their culture and should never be used for eating or greeting another person.

Safety Issues. *Beth and I sat atop the little luge-style sled, speeding down the mountainside after walking the Great Wall of China. We yelped in delight at our first experience on an alpine slide. The Chinese men working there called at us along the way, but as we had no idea what they were saying, we didn't much heed their words.*

Partway down, the thought edged its way into my mind, you know, I bet they don't exactly have OSHA guys here on a regular basis to make sure everything is in tip top working order. And probably, if we got hurt, no personal injury lawyers awaited at the bottom to take my name and number.

But everyone loved the slide, a sightseeing highlight. (Only later did we learn that the yelling men had, apparently, been warning us to slow down.)

Less amusing, to me, was the amusement park we went to with the orphans. Only *after* our kids had ridden the roller coaster did one of the guys mention—"I don't think I'd get on some of these rides. That coaster doesn't look too stable." Once more we realized—this isn't Kansas anymore.

All parents have to judge for themselves the level of safety they'll require. It's a tricky mix of common sense, cultural sensitivity, and faith. But if you go to the developing world expecting to be able to buckle Junior's car seat into a taxi cab, well, good luck finding that safety belt. Expect issues that will challenge you and make you nervous. Some risks you'll take (helmetless bike riding); some you won't (foregoing malaria medications). With small children, particularly, it may be best to work with an established mission family that has experience raising children there.

Children. How does the culture expect children to behave? How does it view children in general? Other cultures might be surprised by the freedom with which American children act and speak. Yet in others ways, their children may be much more independent than ours, having to take greater responsibility at younger ages.

Observe how the children around you behave toward adults. How much do they engage in conversation—or do they not speak unless spoken to? Where do they sit at meals? What acts of deference are expected? What are their daily chores and other responsibilities?

In China, we felt a strange, contradictory mix of attitudes toward children. For urban parents allowed only one child, that child becomes the pearl of the family, lavished with all the attention and opportunity of an only child. But the same attitude can lead to negative ramifications as well.

We saw throw-away children, in a different class because of defects that made them less than what their parents had hoped for. As well, the pressure on the only child to succeed and make the family proud creates a stressful environment for Chinese youth. Tuning in to how the culture views children will help your children avoid being viewed negatively.

Freedom and Individualism. Americans value the individual above all. Other cultures often value community over individual freedom. That's one reason arranged marriages seem so shocking to Americans and not at all to many other cultures. To them, marriage is an act of the family and the community, not just the personal choice of two people. Freedoms we find natural, like giving a friendly hug in public or wearing earrings, they could find offensive. Those we take for granted, your son's wish to dye his hair blue, for example, they may assume will be sacrificed for the greater good.

Be ready to give up personal freedoms you may enjoy at home which could get in the way of acceptance for the group. Your family does not go overseas as individuals but as part of a team, and anything you say or do will reflect on your whole group, because others will look on you as a community. This could apply to the way you dress, spend money, use your free time, display affection in public, and worship.

"You must be careful with this freedom of yours. Do not cause a brother or sister with a weaker conscience to stumble" (1 Corinthians 8:9). Being free in Christ sometimes means being free *not* to claim our rights to freedom. Here we need to follow the physicians' ancient promise—"do no harm."

Personal Questions/Privacy. "Do the women in your country work harder than the men? Chinese women work harder. That is why we look older than our husbands. You look older than your husband—you must work hard like us."

The classroom teacher who quizzed me didn't mean to be insulting. I suspect she considered it an honor to show the evidence of hard work. I smiled and took some refuge in the fact that, yes, I looked dreadful at the moment, because I *felt* dreadful. Then, weakly, I assured her that American women *did* work very hard, and, in fact, I *was* older than my husband, so that must account for it.

Personal questions come with the territory of being, perhaps, the only white American family some people have ever met. Inquiring minds want to know. As I've said, the concepts of privacy and personal space mean different things beyond our borders. Again, community and family are larger than the individual, and knowing the business of everyone in the community helps it function together.

So accept the questions graciously as what they are—sincere attempts to understand you and make you fit into their community. The notion that such close questioning is rude is your American culture talking, not objective fact.

Or you could handle them like Beth did. In a courtyard talking with some neighborhood young people, she sat by Daniel, the 23-year-old guy on our team she'd attached herself to and faithfully adored. Turning to Daniel, one of the young Chinese women asked, "Will you marry me?" Flustered, shy Daniel faltered for an answer to her rather forthright proposal. By no means at a loss, Elizabeth turned to the girl with all her six-year-old indignation and declared, "Hey—I asked him first!" End of *that* discussion.

CHAPTER NINE
REALITY BITES (EMOTIONAL PREPARATION)

Our kids have been to downtown Chicago and seen street people, homeless and seemingly helpless, sitting on curbs, sleeping on benches, slouching in alleys. And yes, they've seen such people even here in their well-manicured suburbs, just more sanitized, as is everything else around here. They are not unaware that the world holds pain. Nonetheless, most American children have not seen firsthand true suffering or hardship. They may know *about* it if, for instance, your family supports a child in Africa or follows world news. But they've never been up close and personal. It takes head knowledge to a vastly different level.

The emotional responses your children have on a mission trip will run the gamut of anger, pity, hopelessness, love, exhaustion, and eagerness. So will yours. But your children won't know that this ricochet is normal. They may feel destabilized and confused. Being prepared can help them remember, when the strong feelings hit, that it's OK to feel strongly. It will also help you channel those feelings into action.

Before You Go

As part of your preparation for the trip, begin weekly discussion times that get everyone talking about their emotional reactions, expectations, and beliefs. Some topics for discussion could include:

—what is one thing I really want to learn/do on this trip?

—why am I going on this trip?

—what is one thing I'm afraid of?

—what spiritual gifts do I think I bring?

—how do I think this trip will affect me?

—what favorite Bible story/verse helps me best prepare for this trip?

—what will I miss most from home?

—what is the difference between pity, sympathy, empathy, and love?

In their book, *Guide to Short-Term Missions*, Mack and Leeann Stiles sum up the goal of serving in the midst of overwhelming need – "God wants soft hearts more than efficient remedies."

Use the issues that bother your children to build them into compassionate Christians who will change injustice rather than sympathetic Christians who feel bad but also helpless. Teach relevant Scripture passages like Isaiah 58 and discuss the tough issues like injustice, racism, and poverty. Brainstorm together what one person can do. Find stories of just one person making a difference. They don't have to be stories of famous people doing great things. Better, actually, are the "average nobodies" just doing their part. One blog I love that chronicled such stories, until the tragic day the writer lost her life in a fire, is http://www.kidscandoit.com/blog/. There, you can find stories of kids the same age as yours, doing things that matter.

Last night our family watched *Remember the Titans* (based on a true story). In it, one young man thought his purpose in life was to play football and lead his high school team to a state championship. When a tragic accident steals his ability to play, he learns his purpose was much greater. Through one young man's courage, an entire town defeated the ugliness and ignorance of racism, while others watched. Just one teen-aged football player, never expecting to change the world, did the right thing, and change happened. If he can, so can your children.

Look, too, at God's use of the "little people." First Corinthians 1:25 explains: "For the foolishness of God is wiser than man's wisdom, and the weakness of God is stronger than man's strength." Have your kids read about David, Gideon, Mary, and Peter, for instance. Why does God seem to absolutely delight in using "the least of these" for his kingdom work?

David was the youngest of Jesse's sons. Gideon's inferiority complex radiates out of Judges 6:15—"My clan is the weakest in Manasseh, and I am the least in my family." Mary lived in the "projects" of Israel and never distinguished herself from any other teenage girl. Peter was an uneducated fishermen with clear signs of ADD.

Repeatedly, we get the message—"It's not who you are; it's who He is through you." In Mother Teresa's words: "We cannot all do great things, but we can all do little things with great love."

Another way to cultivate acts of compassion is to learn all you can about the specific history of the people you will serve. Are they still recovering from the effects of a war? Are there racial issues? Other relevant history?

Wally Mei of Boston has taken his wife and two daughters on missions trips to the Crow Agency in Montana since the youngest was three. Of the emotional impact, he relates, "The most moving part of our experience in the Crow Agency was nursing home visitations. You talk to some of the older women, and their grandfathers were chiefs. They remember what their people went through. They can tell you their stories, and you realize, this is the experience of their people."

We felt that in the Chinese tea shop talking to the lady whose intricate paper cuttings adorned the walls. As she snipped cuttings for us, we learned of her father's torture during the Cultural Revolution. We'd read about it, but now we knew its face and heard, after over 30 years, how much it still hurt. Knowing before we went about that decade of Chinese history made her story more understandable and real than if we had been ignorant of how and why her family and thousands of others had been caught in the schizophrenic chaos of Mao's "cultural cleansing."

Another aid in emotional preparation is to secure an at-home support system for your children. This could be a Sunday school class, school classroom, or youth group. Enlist the kids in the group to commit to praying for your child and encouraging his or her gifts. Arrange for a time when you return for your child to report to this group and tell them of the needs she saw and how she could help. Maybe the group could brainstorm ways for them all to help with a need your child feels strongly about.

Specific Issues Along the Way

Fatigue. Experts in travel books always tell you that the only way to deal with jet leg is to adapt immediately to the new time zone. Don't nap during the day, and go to bed at night even if you're not yet tired. Of course, most of these experts never traveled through twelve time zones with three kids.

Our first night in China the host whisked us off to a theater for a live acrobatic show. The show was both amazing and entertaining. Too bad most of us slept through half of it. But what exactly did they expect would happen when you put 16 jetlagged people who've been awake 24 hours in cushioned seats and turn the lights out?

The only thing worse was the flight home where, because of the time changes, we returned home at the same time we had left China—but our bodies felt 13 hours later! In fact, the experts have a point. You *should* try to adjust right away. Try *not* to sleep during the day. But as always with kids, sometimes compromises have to happen.

During your stay, hard work, unfamiliar conditions, and constant exposure to other people will also bring on fatigue. As a family of five introverts, we find extensive interaction with people exhausting. We need battery recharging time alone. While you are going on this trip to serve others and should anticipate some hardship and sacrifice, ignoring your own needs entirely in the name of service will *decrease* your effectiveness as a missionary. A tired, burnt out, possibly resentful worker doesn't represent Christ well.

Being exhausted will also make you irritable with your children, which won't give them the greatest picture of missionary service. So—don't be afraid to tell your team leader, "I don't think I/the kids can handle going out right now." Pushing yourself can be a good thing. But exhausting yourself won't be. Take time to rest, reconnect, recharge.

Remember, too, that a different climate will bring physical stress. Our team in Costa Rica began distressed that we were not going to be more active, but we soon realized the wisdom of our hosts. Heat saps a lot of energy! They knew we'd wilt after a couple days of hot afternoon activity, and they were right. They understood exactly how much to load on us, even if we did not.

Homesickness. When we left for China, our kids were not yet old enough to really care about e-mail and iPods. Now, a single day without their Facebook lies somewhere between the Titanic and a tsunami in terms of catastrophe. That computer, for today's teens, represents a link with others similar to the sleek Princess phone of our generation.

So when your kids start complaining about the lack of texting and IM capacity in rural Mexico, consider what they're probably really saying. Not, "I can't live without my technology," but "I miss my friends. I feel disconnected. I'm having one of the coolest experiences in my life, and I can't tell my friends about it. What if they forgot me?"

You may have access to an Internet café or something similar. If so, let them take a few minutes to send e-mail or update a Facebook. It will cost a bit, but it will ease their worries. If not, encourage your kids to communicate in other ways. Send postcards (though you'll probably get home before they do). Shop together for inexpensive gifts to bring home to special friends. Have the kids keep journals as if they were writing to a particular friend or friends so they can share the pages with them at home.

Sadness

June sat with her head in our team leader's lap. He stroked her hair while she sat, content. The smile on his lips competed with the sadness in his eyes. Happy he brought her comfort, distressed that her life had been so broken that this small gesture of love was clearly outside the experience of her eight years. New to the orphanage, June rarely spoke and hadn't opened up to the orphanage workers. Now, as the other children ran and played games, she wanted just to feel a "daddy's touch" and find security there. Keith could only guess at the emotional wounds she must carry, and he silently wept over her bent head.

Overwhelming sadness at the hurt they see before their eyes will likely be the greatest emotional challenge for your children. They knew about starving children in Africa, street kids in Brazil, and orphans in China before. But they never met them. Never knew their names. Never been face-to-face with a child whose life story they've known only in novels and infomercials, if at all. They never stood in a dank, dark cave on the side of the sandstone mountain and realized it was someone's home. You can never fully prepare them for this realization, but some things will help.

Help your kids understand God's heart for the poor and weak. Together, read Scriptures that address the subject and talk about it. You'll find sample family Bible studies in appendix B. Assure them, through these passages, that God doesn't forget the hurting. Then, be ready for questions.

Older children will want to know—then why does God allow them to suffer? This may be the first time they've struggled theologically with the problem of suffering. It is important you be honest and not give trite answers. Speak truthfully about how difficult the question is and how people of God have wrestled with it for centuries. Give the best answer you can from your heart, and don't be afraid to say, "I don't know."

Younger children will ask similar questions, but they may ask them in more practical terms. Their concrete minds don't yet run to abstract, "big picture" thoughts of pain and good and evil, but they may ask something like, "Why doesn't Santa visit these kids? I thought he brought toys to everyone." At its heart, it's the same question their older siblings are asking, but in terms a seven-year-old comprehends. (Great, you're saying. Now I have two theological questions on my hands—suffering *and* Santa Claus.)

Teach your children the story of the starfish. You know it – you've heard it in at least one sermon illustration by now. It's the story of the man walking the beach every day picking up starfish and throwing them back into the ocean. Thousands of starfish wash up daily, and he can throw so few back compared to those he cannot help. When an onlooker asks why he does it when he clearly can make no difference at all in the big picture, he replies "It makes a difference to this one," and tosses it back into life.

Help them understand that God doesn't expect them to save all the starfish (though some day they might—who knows?) but to make a difference for that one right now. Keith couldn't save all the orphans in China who had broken hearts and spirits. But it meant the world to June that, on one afternoon, he devoted his time to the simple task of healing one.

Grief. Ten days doesn't seem very long to form bonds of friendship. Who expected Jenny's exuberant smile to still pull at our hearts years later? Who would know shy Lily climbing onto my lap to ride the bus home would be a feeling I still recall so vividly? How could we understand Esther's parting letter, "I may not remember your names, but my heart will remember your faces forever," proudly written in English, would make me tear up even now?

No amount of hardship or sickness on the trip equaled the pain of saying "goodbye." If your experience is like ours, your kids will never have felt so unconditionally loved in their lives as they do by the other children they come to serve. It will be hard to let go.

That's OK. Crying over goodbyes didn't bother the Apostle Paul, so it must be OK. You'll find some ideas for helping your children keep their feelings alive after they get home and channeling them into action in chapter eleven. Let them use their grief to continue making a difference after they've physically said goodbye.

Reverse Culture Shock. When they do come home, your kids will want to tell everyone about their life-changing experience. But life will have gone on as usual for their friends, and few will understand what your kids desperately want to communicate.

Re-entry into American culture will shock kids again, because now they will see our conspicuous consumption with new eyes and won't be as comfortable with its excesses. For a while, at least. We do tend to readjust all too quickly to having all we need and want.

Again, assure kids that feeling "homesick" for the other country and "out of step" with home are normal. More thoughts on how to cope with these feelings are also in chapter eleven.

Your most important trip preparation, however, won't be done with your computer, books, forms, and hands. It will be the preparation you do on your knees.

CHAPTER TEN
PACKING JESUS
(SPIRITUAL PREPARATION)

"Met some new friends last night. Went to their room and read a book that belongs to our friend, John. Our father had a big party. Please talk to the man upstairs about us. Love... ."

We hoped the e-mail would make sense to our church friends back home. I hadn't really spoken in code since playing detective as a 10-year-old. Who knew a 40-year-old suburban gymnastics mom (no, not soccer) would have to learn international spy techniques? Sitting in the hotel lobby typing away at the e-mails, I felt like the mom in *Spy Kids*. Translated into plain English, the message read something like: "Went to Bible study on Gospel of John this evening. We met some new people there who gave their lives to Christ. Please pray for us."

But we couldn't say that. All electronic transmissions in China pass before government eyes. Any reference to Jesus, Bible, prayer, or God could have endangered our hosts, the Bible study students, and our agency's future. So, coded e-mails. Your kids will *love* that. Finally, some *real* excitement. They'll be all set to break into their detective sets. Of course, the stakes make it no game of pretend.

With all the frenzy of packing, passports, fundraising, and letter writing, it's easy to forget the unseen, intangible preparation. Yet to overlook this is to forget that your biggest battles will not be physical but spiritual. If Satan can't keep you from going on a mission trip, he'll definitely try to keep your focus distracted with details rather than on spiritual preparation.

So, from the beginning, retain that focus with regular prayer time. Let your children see that you know Ephesians 6:12 is real life, not just a Bible verse.

Since you're going on a *family* mission trip, your prayer preparation time is a great place to begin involving the kids in spiritual leadership. Allow all family members to rotate responsibility for leading the prayer time rather than making it all parent-generated. By going, you're telling them they're old enough to minister—show you believe it. If the littlest ones need help, team them with an older sibling.

Each time you pray, remember several aspects of your preparation. Your prayers will include concerns about fundraising, physical health and safety, smooth functioning of details, your own spiritual readiness, and the needs of the people you meet. Some ideas to include:

⊙ Make time for everyone to share their concerns for prayer. No concern from anyone is too small.

⊙ Suggest Bible verses that may address particular concerns.

◉ Have the leader look up facts on the internet about the country or the particular people you will meet that could be important points to pray about, (i.e., percentage of Christians in the population, religious persecution, poverty, etc.). Get as specific as you can. Had we known which orphanage we would be visiting, we could have gone on their website at home and "met" all of the children and prayed for them individually. For various reasons, the agency could not let us know, but you may have the ability to get very detailed information for prayer.

◉ Pray for fundraising, along with prayers of thanks for people who have supported you and intercession for them. Let kids see that support is a two-way street.

◉ Pray for the other members of your team. Here, too, kids need to see that teamwork begins *before* the actual work, and mutual support wins spiritual battles.

◉ Pray for details of the trip, small and large.

◉ Pray for health and safety of all involved.

◉ Pray for each person's part in ministry. Mention each family member by name, and pray for his or her spiritual gifts to be used by God.

"A spiritual gift is given to each of us as a means of helping the entire church" (I Corinthians 12:7). Did you know that includes six-year-olds? Your children have spiritual gifts—do they know what they are? Do you? While it's not necessary to find out your spiritual gifts to go on a short-term mission trip (you'll be asked to do all kinds of things outside your comfort zone. Remember? Be flexible!), knowing encourages your kids to believe they can have an impact.

Older children can take these spiritual inventory tests themselves. For younger ones, perhaps your own observations remain the best barometer. Look at the sets of questions in Appendix A and ask yourself if you see any of these things standing out in your child. You may need to talk about different gifts to make sure the kids understand their meaning. Telling a child she has the gift of discernment may not register at all, since the word isn't one she commonly uses. Instead, tell her you think she has a special ability to see right from wrong and understand people more deeply than the average person.

After you've talked about what each gift means, spend some time brainstorming how they might use their gifts on a mission. Some ideas our kids saw in their gifts: Encouragement—I could tell the orphans what a good job they're doing in school learning English. Discernment—I could see what was *really* keeping a person from accepting Jesus and talk about it. Leadership—I could organize games and songs and make sure everyone is included.

Sensitive Spiritual Issues

Issues of spiritual freedom may confuse your children, since they probably can't conceive of living somewhere where mentioning Jesus could get someone put in jail. Sure, they studied the Pilgrims in elementary school, but probably the watered-down version (you know—the one where the Pilgrims fled England for no real reason and then gave thanks to, um, the Indians, for helping them out?).

But real religious persecution in today's world? They are mercifully clueless. (So are a lot of adults, not so mercifully.) Teenagers may have a better grasp, having grappled with Mideast history class and Darfur, but the knowledge remains distant.

"Mom, what was Isaiah* talking about? Why was he in jail? Don't only bad people go to jail?"

Emily's 11-year-old worldview couldn't quite account for this seeming aberration. Bad people got punished with jail; good people didn't.

Yet there our Chinese guide had sat an hour ago, explaining in quiet tones why he had been slow to join us.

"They broke into our house church. Again. I wasn't in jail so long this time. Only two weeks. Next time, it will probably be worse." Next time? He spoke calmly of the certainty of it.

"No. Not always. In some places, very good people go to jail. Jesus got thrown in jail, remember? And so did Paul and Peter. In some places, people just don't want to hear about Jesus. And they don't want anyone else to. Isaiah is a very good man who loves Jesus."

"That's not fair."
"No. The world really isn't sometimes."

(*Name has been changed)

I'm going to assume you're not taking your kids somewhere they could get shot for saying they love Jesus. I can't quite imagine an agency agreeing to a "family" trip under those circumstances. Any mistakes in areas you go to, therefore, probably endanger the nationals in the country and the future of your agency's presence there more than yourselves.

Often, though, what can and can't be said isn't all that black and white. We could not, for instance, openly talk about our faith to the orphans. We could not present our faith when we went to visit various public school classrooms. We could, however, answer questions students posed. If they asked why we cared about orphans, we could tell them because Jesus cared and we were his followers. If they asked, "Do you believe in God?" we could answer. But we couldn't bring up the subject ourselves. Truly, we were free to follow Peter's advice: "If you're asked about your Christian hope, always be ready to explain it" (I Peter 3:15) — *if* someone asked.

In a typical junior high question-and-answer session, Chinese teens asked us standard questions: "What's your favorite color?" (blue), "What is your work?" (writer, doctor), "What do you like best about China?" (you!), or "Do you know Michael Jordan?" (um, no. Sorry.) Amid these now-expected queries, one boy raised his hand. I called on him.

"Do you hate Osama bin Laden?" Wow. The eager, noisy classroom hushed. I struggled for an answer. Remember, this was October, 2002.

"Well, I hate what Osama bin Laden has done. I hate anyone hurting the innocent, and I wish for him to come to justice. But no, I do not hate him. Jesus tells me to love everyone and pray for my enemies as He did. And I try to follow Him."

In response to one of the most difficult questions we encountered, I sensed we had just crossed some invisible line of credibility. Unschooled in forgiveness, those students witnessed a "realness" to Christians they had to think about. We didn't spread the gospel, hand out tracts, or open-air preach. We just answered questions. Sometimes, when God shows up at the Q & A, that's quite enough.

Spiritual Support

While your kids complete all their preparation for a mission trip, they probably don't perceive the situations they're learning about as part of a bigger "spiritual" picture. To them, issues of health, language, fundraising, or culture occupy distinct departments and can be addressed in simple, practical terms. In fact, they *should* be addressed that way on one level. But another level to your journey can't be seen in black and white, or even living color. It can't be *seen* at all. So put on a pair of those cereal-box 3D glasses and call them "spiritual domain" glasses. Then ask your kids to look through them to see their real obstacles.

"For we are not fighting against people made of flesh and blood, but against evil rulers and authorities of the unseen world, against those mighty powers of darkness who rule this world, and against wicked spirits in the heavenly realms" (Ephesians 6:12).

Any time a Christian seeks to move God's kingdom forward, Satan will counter. You're seeking to do something that will

1) help others in need,

2) spread the gospel of Jesus, and

3 (perhaps most dangerous) profoundly affect the next generation of Christian leaders (your children).

Satan will not sit back and TiVo the action. What a great opportunity for your children to learn the real-life application of Ephesians 6:12!

Talk with your kids about preparation for battle. Before a soldier goes off to war, what would he or she do? Basic training—that's a lot of what you've already been through in this book. But there's more. Can a soldier fight a war alone? If your kids think long enough, they should come up with dozens of ways other people support the efforts of one soldier. Who runs training camp? Who signs the paycheck? Who pays the taxes for his salary? Who sews her uniform? Who mines the metal that goes to the factory that makes his tank? Who recruits comrades to fight beside her?

In the same way, kids can realize they need a support team back home to help them fight the good fight on a mission trip. Besides including kids in the activities of your general support list, give them opportunities to form their own base. Request that your child be able to present her trip plans for Sunday school class, youth group, or a Christian school classroom. Maybe you could create prayer cards or some other small trinket for them to pass out to ask other kids to be part of their prayer team. Not only are your kids involved in missions; now, a roomful of others can join in.

Not all countries will oppose Christianity by any means. In some mission sites, you can't speak openly about your faith. Sometimes, however, you'll be asked to! So may your kids. Will they be comfortable sharing their faith?

The Latin word testis originally meant 'witness.' It comes from the roots tre, meaning 'three,' and sta, meaning 'stand.' A witness was "a third person standing by." From that came the verb testificare 'to bear witness,' which evolved into Middle English 'testify' in the fourteenth century. All this to explain--a testimony is our way of saying "I have stood and watched what God has done, and I am willing to go on record and tell you what I know."

Together, anticipate some questions people might ask, and help one another formulate an individual testimony about what Jesus means in your lives. Everyone's will be different, as they should be.

Think about some basic questions—why am I a Christian? How did I become one? Who is Jesus to me? How has he changed me? What is he doing in my life right now?

Memorize fundamental verses together that explain the gospel. A common choice is what we call The Romans Road—Romans 310, 3:23, 6:23, 5:8, 10:9, and 10:13. Others add Romans 5:1, 8:1 and 8:38-39 to "complete" the salvation story. You don't need a polished speech but a simple, concise answer to the questions—what do you believe about God and why? What difference does it made? You'll find some tips for writing a positive testimony in Appendix G.

So how do you convey the gospel without words in an area where you can't speak openly? "In everything you do, stay away from complaining and arguing, so that no one can speak a word against you. Let your light shine brightly before them" (Philippians 2:14-15). "Love each other. Just as I have loved you, you should love each other. Your love for one another will prove to the world that you are my disciples" (John 13:34-35). "Preach the gospel at all times—If necessary, use words." (St Francis of Asissi).

By treating those you serve with love and respect, you plant seeds that resident missionaries and/or nationals can harvest. Do the part God has given you—and He'll take care of the rest.

CHAPTER ELEVEN
YOU CAN'T GO HOME AGAIN

"Mom, when can we go back?" Considering we'd barely boarded the plane to go home, I hadn't really thought quite that far ahead. The question, however, encouraged me that we had succeeded in cultivating hearts for the world. Those 35 children there will forever be part of our three children here. But how, now that suburban life again threatens to engulf us with its often-false urgencies and complacencies, can we ensure lessons learned won't be forgotten?

Remembering can begin in small ways. Two months after our return, the three girls opened a new type of Christmas gift. Their small envelopes contained red and green cards, each of them displaying the same picture and "Samaritan's Purse" written across the front, each of them a puzzle to the girls at first. What on earth could they be getting in this nondescript envelope and card?

Inside, the typed script informed them that "A gift has been given in your honor to care for an orphan for a month." Unlike the standard tossed-among-the-paper greeting card, these cards remained protectively in their laps. Later, all three placed their treasured cards on the TV cabinet, where they would see them standing every day, and began wondering where "their" orphan lived.

Now an annual tradition, the girls (and their dad) look forward to finding out what they have done every Christmas to help someone else.

Samaritan's Purse, World Vision, Heifer International and others put out similar "gift catalogs" each year for people to selects "gifts" such as these for their loved ones. Other simple things, too, can keep your family connected to their mission after they return.

- ✗ Keep a journal on your trip. Let everyone contribute. Continue to write in it after your return, recording your reactions to coming home and your hopes for future missions. Go back and read sections together from time to time to remember and talk about those times.

- ✗ Continue regular prayer times for the area and people you visited.

- ✗ Put together a scrapbook of your trip with pictures, mementos, journal writing, ticket stubs, etc.

- ✗ Keep in touch with those you touched. At home, we continued to e-mail some of the children we met, through the orphanage website. Now, we also support one of them monthly. The girls have enjoyed watching some of the Chinese kids grow and progress, like Esther, then a shy young teen, now pursuing an Art degree at the University. The girls know this opportunity for study would never have come to her before her rescue by the orphanage.

- ✗ Create presentations for your supporters. Prepare a five to ten minute talk for church with contributions from everyone in the family. Emily created a PowerPoint presentation she could use for Sunday school, and she later showed it to her 4H group as well. Let others see the faces, names, and stories of those they sent you to help.

- ✗ Remember to send out a post-trip letter telling your supporters about your ministry.

- ✗ Find opportunities to tell others about what you did. Not only your church but service organizations, Bible studies, classrooms, and other groups may enjoy hearing your stories. A nearby college could have an InterVarsity or Campus Life group excited to learn of your opportunity. A Christian school, even one your children don't attend, may enjoy the chance to have your kids tell about their adventures. A public class room that may be studying the region you visited can also benefit, as long as you remained sensitive to religion-in-schools issues.

- ✗ Start a blog on your trip and continue it when you return, offering readers insight into why you went, what you saw and did, and what they can learn and do.

Telling the story of what you did, however, only opens the chapter of what you *can* do. Your impact overseas doesn't need to end when you touch down home. As you tell others about your trip, you have the perfect opportunity to encourage their involvement as well. First, as a family that has gone on a short-term mission and lived to tell about it, you serve as proof that they can do it, too. Your family can be emissaries to move others toward the same experience. Maybe you could even spearhead the next group to go!

Second, you can inform others of the needs you left behind and mobilize them into action. What can they continue to do, after supporting you, to see that those you served together continue to benefit? Our supporters could continue to donate directly to the orphanage, if they chose.

→ Arrange events that support the initiatives you took part in. Organize a rummage sale, garden walk, or pasta night that contributes its proceeds to digging wells, performing cleft palate surgery, or building homes. As your kids work to serve spaghetti or label sale items, they not only raise money but physically serve once more.

→ Find volunteer activities at home. If World Relief, an organization that helps settle refugees in America, has a presence in your area, they always need volunteers to help others adjust to life in the US. Love, Inc. also connects volunteers to multiple opportunities. Community colleges, libraries, or local churches may be in need of ESL teachers, after-school tutors, or child care for parents taking courses. Whatever you do, don't let the "hands on" end when you open your own front door. A great site for finding family volunteer ideas at home is: http://pinterest.com/AmyLSullivan/.

→ Follow others missionaries. Your church probably has a list of missionaries they support. Track them and pray for them. Maybe you can choose one that serves near the area you visited or that has a family makeup like yours and send them packages and letters of encouragement.

→ Take a day each month to eat a Chinese meal (or Mexican, Indian, Appalachian, etc.) and talk about current events there. You can bet our kids raced to make sure "their" kids were safe after the '08 earthquake in China. They paid much closer attention to world events when they felt closer to the world.

→ Plan your next trip!

Our girls love taking part in two regular programs now, Operation Christmas Child and The Box Project. As do many families, every Christmas each girl packs a shoe box for another child full of small gifts and necessities. They choose the age and gender of the child themselves as well as the box contents, within guidelines.

Another box they pack, this one monthly, goes to a family in Mississippi matched to us by The Box Project. This organization targets the rural poor in the US and matches them to a donor who promises to send them a box (or gift certificate) monthly, filled with things they need and want. Our "family" has four girls, so packing a birthday box elicits an excited run around Target or Walmart for our kids. The project also allows the girls to correspond. Not only can our daughters learn of each others' worlds, but ours can encourage hers that they can finish school, go to college, and break out of poverty.

Of course, you *can* go home again. Physically. But mentally, emotionally, spiritually? I hope not. I hope for you, as I do for us, you will never view American consume/dispose culture as status quo. I hope you'll never again see suffering people across the globe as endless numbers. I hope you'll never forget that Jesus looks a lot like a Chinese orphan with a cleft palate. When you return, you'll have your own picture to insert there. That's good. Because it's just possible, your adventure will have only begun when you touch down at home again.

Appendix A

Sample Spiritual Gift Inventory

Look at the statements after each heading. Do you agree or disagree with them? If you agree with about 75 percent, you may have a spiritual gift in that area.

Please understand that this is not an exhaustive list of all the spiritual gifts, nor is it a scientific assessment. It includes mainly those gifts that people may not know they have or understand fully. If you have the gift of tongues, for instance, chances are you know it and don't need to take an inventory. Leadership, on the other hand, is much more difficult to discern. If you want to take a more formal inventory, try websites such as: www.kodachrome.org/spiritgift; www.timshen.truepath.com/inventory; or www.goingthedistance.org.

Exhortation

Speaking in front of people doesn't bother me.

I enjoy explaining ideas from the Bible.

When I speak, people often listen and agree.

I am able to take a difficult passage in the Bible and explain it so people can understand.

I enjoy taking time to study the Bible and learn what it really means.

People have told me my writing has challenged them to better discipleship.

People have told me I taught something that changed their outlook or way of living.

I can motivate people to follow God more closely through my words.

I feel energized by being in front of a group and speaking God's word.

I can take challenging truths and explain them in a way that makes people accept the challenge instead of rebel against it.

Serving

I enjoy helping out in the church.

I enjoy doing the "little things" for people.

I don't mind when my work goes unnoticed. I don't care who gets credit.

I like to do "behind the scenes" help.

I don't think I have special talents; I just do what needs to get done.

I often end up in positions assisting leaders, not leading myself.

I really like to participate in service projects at school, church, scouts., etc.

People tell me they couldn't get things done without me.

When I help set up, clean up, etc. I feel like I've served God.

When someone is hurt or sad, I try to find practical things I can do to help.

Teaching

I can present a Bible lesson in a way people find interesting.

I enjoy studying the Bible to get new things out of it.

People have told me I helped them understand the Bible better.

I can make difficult things easy to understand.

I like to write thoughts and feelings that help other people understand things.

Friends often turn to me for homework help if they don't understand something.

I enjoy teaching Sunday school to younger kids.

I enjoy showing others how to do something.

I have a heart to help Christians who have lost their way.

I feel effective in the discipling of other believers.

Encouraging

People often come to me with their problems.

I like to help people become better at what they are doing.

I enjoy building other people up.

I can get people to do their jobs willingly.

When people are discouraged I love to give them words of hope.

I can challenge others to improve without making them feel like losers.

I have spoken words that gave confidence to people unsure of their faith or in trouble.

If someone is losing faith that she can do something, I enjoy helping her keep going.

I get a lot of satisfaction out of seeing someone succeed after I feel I've said or done something to help.

I see gifts in other people and love to help them get better at those things.

Discernment

I can recognize when something is evil.

It is easy to me to sense whether a person is honest or dishonest.

I sometimes feel like I know exactly what God wants to do in certain times and places.

I am able to understand difficult portions of God's word.

I can clearly see the strategies that have seemed to work best in the past in God's work.

I can often guide a person to the best solution to a problem.

When I hear someone make a theological statement, I am a good judge of its truth.

I feel that I have a special insight in selecting the best alternative in a difficult situation.

I can quickly recognize whether or not a person's teaching is consistent with God's word.

People turn to me when they don't know whether or not to believe something.

Evangelism

I am attracted to non-believers.

I like to tell others about Jesus.

I have led others to a decision for salvation through faith in Christ.

Starting a new church or mission energizes me.

I minister better to nonbelievers than to believers.

God seems to give me the right words when I tell others about Jesus.

I can explain the gospel clearly.

I know how to find a way to naturally talk about God with someone.

I have far more nonChristian friends than Christian ones.

I can adapt well to other cultures and mindsets in order to relate to people.

Mercy

When I see people in need, I really want to help them.

I feel great compassion for the problems of others.

I enjoy caring for those who have physical or mental problems.

I enjoy spending time with someone who is otherwise alone.

I enjoy visiting in hospitals, retirement homes, or prisons.

If someone is facing a crisis, I enjoy helping them.

I notice if someone seems lonely or sad.

I feel compassion and want to do something when I hear news stories about people being treated badly.

I sometimes find myself overextended in volunteering for service organizations.

I always want to help when I hear of a need.

Hospitality

I like having people drop by my house when I don't expect them.

My home is always open to anyone God brings my way.

I enjoy greeting people at our church.

I try to make everyone feel welcome and comfortable at social events.

When people come to my home, they often say they feel at home there.

I am a person people say they can be themselves around.

I don't care that much about what my home looks like, as long as it's full of people.

I've always got time to listen.

I sometimes have people living with me who aren't actually relatives.

People just seem to know my house is a place of refuge.

Leadership

Others are willing to follow my guidance to accomplish things.

I have been responsible for guiding tasks in my church to success.

I am able to delegate tasks to others.

I can facilitate getting others to use their gifts to solve a problem.

I can motivate people to get involved.

I can recognize talents in others and find ways of using them.

God has given me a position of authority over different groups.

People sometimes look to me for guidance in coordination, organization, and ministry opportunities.

People seem to respect me when I take the lead.

I enjoy creating a vision for a project and getting people on board.

Giving

I give sacrificially because I know that God will meet my needs.

I choose to live a simple lifestyle so my "things" won't get in the way of my service.

God has used me when someone had a financial need.

A big house, hefty savings, or the right clothes just don't matter to me.

I have felt God leading me to give money to a particular person or organization.

I am not jealous of those who have more material possessions than I do.

I do believe that everything I have belongs to God.

I enjoy meeting needs and seek out ways to do so.

I would rather do without something I want if I think I could give something someone else really needed.

I can't throw anything away without asking first, "Could someone use this?"

Faith

I am convinced God will do what He promised, even when I don't see it.

I stand firm in my personal beliefs even when others make fun of them.

My hope in God inspires to others.

I am ready to try the impossible because I know God won't fail.

I often encourage others with my positive attitude.

I don't really question the 'how' of something if I feel God wants it done.

Reading Hebrews 11 give me a boost every time, even the tough parts.

I don't really fear taking risks when I believe God is in it.

My ability to trust God in difficult times encourages others to stand firm as well.

I have seen so many exciting things from God in the past; it's not hard to trust Him with my future.

Prayer

I enjoy praying for others.

I find myself praying when even when other things are begging for my attention.

When I hear a prayer request, I pray for that need immediately and continually.

My first thought when someone expresses a need is to pray.

I take the lead in establishing a prayer chain at church.

I I pray for people I don't know regularly.

I hate it when people say, "well, all we can do now is pray." I know that's the first thing we should do!

I read missionary reports and other things to find out how to pray more effectively.

People have told me that my prayers for them are effective.

People have expressed special gratitude for my prayers.

Appendix B

Family Bible Study — Isaiah 58

Getting started: Introduce your kids to the "Rube Goldberg machine." Basically, this is defined as a complex machine using everyday materials to perform an easy activity in a series of complicated steps. Think the game "Mousetrap." View together a video clip of such a machine or the cartoons that inspired them. Some of these can be found at rubegoldberg.com and mousetrapcontraptions.com. Others may be located by just googling "Rube Goldberg machine." Talk about all the steps involved and what would happen if one step didn't work. If you feel creative, make a machine of your own. Then, discuss Isaiah 58. Adapt the questions to your kids' ages.

vs. 1-4.

1. How is God feeling in these first four verses? How do you know?

2. What pictures does He give of what the people are doing?

3. At whom is He angry?

4. Why is God angry?

5. What sins are the leaders of this country committing?

6. Have you ever hurt someone else because of the way you acted? What did that do to your relationship? Did things feel wrong? What did you do?

Explain: When one person behaves selfishly, another often gets hurt. It works with three-year-olds and with entire countries and our world. If a country's leaders are selfish, people will suffer. If one country behaves selfishly toward another country, people will suffer. It's just like when you hurt a friend. God loves him. It's not his fault. But he got hurt. It hurts God when people are selfish, but He allows us to be free to choose badly if we wish. Unfortunately, it knocks everything out of order if we do, and that's how a lot of suffering in the world happens. We've chosen to mess up the perfect system for everyone in order to get more for "me." If someone messes up just one step in God's perfect process for taking care of everyone, the entire machine can break down.

Vs. 5-12

7. Why do the people suffer?

8. Does God want them to?

9. What does God want the leaders to do?

10. What result does He promise?

11. How does God want suffering to end? (i.e. — What can we do ourselves?)

Words to remember: He has showed you, O man, what is good. And what does the Lord require of you? To act justly and to love mercy and to walk humbly with your God. (Micah 6:8, NIV)

Family Bible Study—I Corinthians 1:18-31

How big do we have to be to serve God? Can one person make a difference?

Getting started: Use video clips to tell the story of the "little people." If you have older children, *The Lord of the Rings* movies are a great choice for teaching the importance of being willing more than being big or smart. Focus on a few clips of Merry and his brave story.

For younger kids, Veggie Tales' "Gideon—Tuba Warrior" makes a good choice.

Discussion questions: What is Merry/Gideon's problem? What are some of his positive qualities? How does he prove the worth of "the little people"?

Read the Corinthians passage.

1. What mental picture does the word "foolish" put into your head?

2. Why is the message of the cross foolish sounding?

3. What is the difference between being smart and being wise?

*Smart—that means knowing a lot.

*Wise—that means knowing the right way to use what you know—and doing it.

4. Who were most of the first Christians? (v26) (Some translations call these people "the nothings of the world—those that in the eyes of the world do not exist.") Why? If God chose people in your school, neighborhood, etc. whom might He choose?

5. What's the *big picture* reason He does things that way?

6. How might God use you, no matter how old you are?

7. What do you think you have to do to be used by God?

Jesus didn't want people to believe they could be saved, forgiven, and changed because of who *they* were. He wanted them to remember—"no one does good, not even one" (Romans 3:12). That's why he was willing to let His message sound foolish to people who insisted they were smart enough or good enough on their own. He knew they needed to become a little less full of themselves before they could be full of Him.

Have each person take a couple of minutes to fill in these blanks and then talk about them.

I don't think you can use me God because I'm too _____.

I don't think you can use me God because I'm not _____.

I don't think you can use me God because I can't _____.

How might God use exactly that "problem" in a good way?

Ex: "I'm too shy." Maybe your compassion for people in embarrassing situations will be a great help to someone sometime.

Words to remember:

"My gracious favor is all you need. My power works best in your weakness."

(2 Corinthians 9:12)

Appendix C

Sample Packing List

Shoes
- water sandals
- hiking/walking shoes

For many tropical countries, you'll want a pair of shoes that can get wet and one you will *always* keep dry. If the hiking/gym shoes get wet, they may never, ever dry until you get home. That, believe me, is not comfortable.

Clothes
- 4 T-shirts, one or two long sleeved to protect from mosquitoes, sunburn, and scratches.
- 3 pairs of shorts, if going to a hot climate in a culture where shorts are acceptable.
- 2 pairs of long pants. Jeans are not a good option. They take forever to dry, don't allow for air circulation, and are often not considered nice enough in another culture. Try khakis or something similar.
- Skirts, below the knee, in cultures where this is expected of women
- Underwear
- Socks
- Pajamas
- Jacket--preferably a water repellant one
- Hat. You need sun protection! Be sure to protect your neck as well.
- Laundry bag

*Often, people bring clothes they plan to leave behind. That frees up return luggage as well as helping the local people.

First Aid
- insect repellant!!
- band aids
- diarrhea treatment
- motion sickness medicine
- anti-bacterial ointment
- pain relievers/fever reducers
- sunscreen
- aloe gel for sunburn
- anti-histamine tablets, for allergic reactions, stings, etc.
- prescription drugs in original containers

Toiletries
- razor
- toothbrush with cover and toothpaste
- shampoo and conditioner
- brush or comb
- antiperspirant
- tampons
- toilet paper/tissue
- vitamins
- contact solutions
- extra pair of glasses and contacts with case
- face/body wash/soap
- your own washcloth. These are often not provided overseas, even in hotel rooms. They are considered personal items, not linens.

Miscellaneous
- cash, in smaller bills. In many places, bills larger than $20 are considered suspect and may not be accepted.

Also, many countries accept only crisp new American bills. Before leaving, ask the bank for new bills with no tears, ink marks, etc.

- micro LED flashlight
- pocket knife, scissors (not in carry on!)
- zip ties
- sunglasses
- small bottle of laundry detergent
- earplugs
- lighter
- pens and journal
- gifts for your hosts
- water purification system, where needed
- nail file
- super glue
- clothesline
- sewing thread and needles
- water bottle
- camera
- ziploc bags
- plug adapters
- a Xerox of your passport, drivers license, credit cards, airline tickets, and any reservations that you've prepaid. Leave a copy of these at home with your emergency contact as well.
- emergency contact information (your names, addresses and phone numbers, emergency contact number at home, and those of physicians at home.)
- health forms, including immunization record, physician contact information, allergies, and medical conditions.

Unpacking List (What you don't need to take)

- Unneeded electronics. One cell phone, if it works there, and maybe a laptop/tablet to communicate with home and do needed research. Otherwise, leave anything else at home.
- Keys. Get a ride to the airport, and leave your keys with someone at home.
- Wallet. If you're going to carry your wallet, leave most of its contents at home. Better, take a money belt with the few things you'll need.
- Purse. Just no, ladies. There is nothing you need that badly.
- jewelry
- cosmetics

Appendix D

Sample Parental Approval Form

PARENTAL/GUARDIAN APPROVAL FOR MINOR TO TRAVEL AND MEDICAL AUTHORIZATION

IN WITNESS WHEREOF AND BY SIGNING BELOW, I APPROVE TRAVEL FOR MY CHILD AS FOLLOWS:

NAME_____
(Child's Name)

AGED_____
(Child's Age)

TRAVELING
TO_____
(Destination or Type of Travel)

FROM _____TO_____
(Departure Date) (Return Date)

WITH _____
(Traveling Adult's Full Name)

I ALSO AUTHORIZE THE TRAVELING ADULT TO OBTAIN ANY NECESSARY MEDICAL TREATMENT BY A LICENSED PHYSICIAN/ HOSPITAL/PHARMACY/ RESCUE SQUAD/ AMBULANCE COMPANY / MEDICAL AIR EVACUATION COMPANY.

IN THE EVENT THE TRAVELING ADULT IS INCAPACITATED AND CANNOT GIVE AUTHORIZATION FOR TREATMENT, I AUTHORIZE A LICENSED PHYSICIAN/ HOSPITAL/ PHARMACY/ RESCUE SQUAD, AMBULANCE COMPANY /MEDICAL AIR EVACUATION COMPANY TO GIVE MY CHILD ANY NECESSARY MEDICAL TREATMENT.

SIGNATURES:

_____
Legal Mother Printed Name

_____
Signature

_____
Legal Father Printed Name

_____
Signature

I, hereby certify that _____
and/or_____ (Legal Mother, Father or Guardian) (Legal Mother, Father or Guardian) personally appeared before me and executed this document giving permission for the child(ren) named above to travel out of the United States of America with the Traveling Adult named above. This document also includes authorization of medical treatment for the child if necessary. I attest that this instrument is executed willingly and voluntarily, without being coerced, by the above signor(s), and it is their free act and deed for the purposes of expressing their approval. In the circumstance of one parent or both parents being deceased or that the legal parents do not have child custody, I attest that the surviving parent or legal guardian swore to the accuracy of the death certificate(s) and/or guardianship documents attached to this document in my presence.

Date_____

Notary Public Signature

_____

County of _____

State or Commonwealth of _____

My commission expires _____

Appendix E

Budget Worksheet

Item	Base Rate	x# of family members	Total
Airfare	_____	_____	_____
organization fees	_____	_____	_____
meals	_____	_____	_____
lodging	_____	_____	_____
immunizations	_____	_____	_____
passports	_____	_____	_____
travel insurance	_____	_____	_____
new clothing	_____	_____	_____
medicines	_____	_____	_____
new luggage	_____	_____	_____
transportation (to and from airport)	_____	_____	_____
in-country transportation	_____	_____	_____
exit fees	_____	_____	_____
gifts	_____	_____	_____
tips	_____	_____	_____
photo developing	_____	_____	_____
misc supplies	_____	_____	_____
language learning	_____	_____	_____
donations	_____	_____	_____

TOTAL: _____

Appendix F

Timeline Checklist

Twelve Months Out

_____Choose Your Trip

_____Start language lessons with online resources or local classes

Ten Months Out

_____Start monthly family meetings to talk about what you're learning, what each person is going to be responsible for, special preparation you're going to make, and any questions or concerns. Begin family Bible studies.

_____Begin gathering prayer support

_____Create presentations for fundraising

Eight Months Out

_____Write and send fundraising letters/emails

_____Plan any fundraising events

Six Months Out

_____Purchase airfare, if not done by agency

_____Apply for passports

_____Check on traveler's insurance coverage

_____Start immunization process

Two Months Out

_____Schedule a commissioning service for your family at your church

One Month Out

_____Purchase gifts for hosts and other supplies you plan to bring

_____Buy needed items like new clothing, money belt, and medicines

_____Photocopy passport, credit cards, and identification and leave with a responsible person. Fill out medical emergency forms detailing medical history and allergies of each family member., leaving one of these home as well.

_____Work out transportation details to and form the airport

One Week Out

_____Pack, to make sure you don't have too much

Appendix G

TESTIMONY TIPS

A well written personal testimony:
- is easy and natural to use in conversation
- is proof that God is alive and active in your life
- gives evidence of its truth
-
- A poorly written testimony:
- runs too long
- focuses on a sinful past
- is vague
- does not tell how God is work in our life now
- uses stories that only Americans can relate to

General Structure

Begin with an engaging introduction. Include thanking God for the opportunity to be with them, a greeting in their language, or something you are enjoying about their country.

Think of a testimony as a series of pictures that show God in your life. Tell your audience what those pictures look like.

Some of those pictures:

- Your life, thoughts, priorities or relationships before believing in Jesus
- How you came to believe in Jesus
- Your life, thoughts, priorities or relationships since believing in Jesus
- How God has made a difference in your life recently

- How you expect God to continue leading your future
- How He led you on this trip

Brainstorm

- Take 10 minutes to write down ideas that could be included.
- Think of an stories from your life that could illustrate your points. Make sure people of another culture can understand those stories.

Write

Take 15 minutes to gather ideas into an outline. Aim for a 3-minute testimony. Avoid complex sentences, word plays, puns, idioms, and Christian slang.

Make sure your translator understands what you are saying. Be patient if he has questions. If possible, write out a copy and give it to him ahead of time so he can translate it in writing. Ask how often he would like you to stop for translation. Finally, be sure to give him a public thank you.

Appendix H

Sample Support Letter

Dear _____,

I am excited to share with my family and friends how God has given me/us the opportunity to share in a mission trip to Costa Rica this December. About twelve members of our church, _____, plan to travel over Christmas break to work in _____, a town on the Nicaraguan border, one of the poorest areas of the country.

Though Costa Rica is considered the most advanced country in Central America, the people who have come across the border still live in temporary housing, lacking health care, school needs, and employment. They are not included or well-accepted in society.

We will be partnering with a local church to work in construction, medicine, music and drama, children's ministry, and any other needs they may have to bring God's love to a marginalized people. We leave _____ and return to the States _____, a group of changed people who have made a change in others' lives!

This is a team project—and you are needed on my team! I am asking that you support our team with your prayers, as this is the most essential part of our success. We cannot go without a solid support of prayer surrounding us.

Also, we need financial support to cover both our costs and the cost of materials for the work we will be doing. We are needing to raise _____ per person for our ten-day trip. If you are able to donate any part of this amount, we would be greatly blessed and appreciative.

Please make checks payable to _____ and send to my address, or donate online at _____ making a notation that the funds are for my Costa Rica support. Your gift is tax deductible. Please *do not* make a check out to me, as that would no longer be deductible.

Thank you for your caring and support.

_____I would love to pray for your support!
_____ I would love to donate toward your work.
_____ $25 _____ $50 _____ $100 _____ any amount

www.ingramcontent.com/pod-product-compliance
Lightning Source LLC
Chambersburg PA
CBHW061327040426
42444CB00011B/2811